The Calling

George Patton Bargas

authorHOUSE®

AuthorHouse™
1663 Liberty Drive
Bloomington, IN 47403
www.authorhouse.com
Phone: 833-262-8899

Published by AuthorHouse 02/06/2023

ISBN: 979-8-8230-0036-9 (sc)
ISBN: 979-8-8230-0034-5 (hc)
ISBN: 979-8-8230-0035-2 (e)

Library of Congress Control Number: 2023902002

Print information available on the last page.

Contents

Introduction

These are the accounts of my life and my war against God that lasted more than forty years. To understand this, you must first understand Book One. Book one was my first publication, titled "The Journey". Book One was written more than 50 years ago. It speaks of my experiences in the jungles of Vietnam...... the physical battles as well as the mental and Spiritual battles.

I waited many years to put it into publication because It was extremely painful for me to read and have to remember. When I finally sent it for publication, 50 years later... it went through the various departments, as all books do. It finally got to the cover design department and a copy of the cover was E-mailed to me for my approval..... I was outraged! The cover was very similar to the cover designed for "Footprints in The Sand", a Christian poem. Mine was a gruesome book. A book which relates my hate and anger towards God. A book of war, bloodshed and vengeance. A book about a man who became what he hated most .... and I expected the cover to express that. I spent many sleepless nights wrestling with the design of this cover. I know the man that designed it must have read it in order to get an idea for the cover. How could he possibly have come up with that kind of cover.

I called my Pastor and expressed my anger and that I felt betrayed by God .... Again! One night, as I sat, still brooding over the cover and trying to understand, something happened. I received a message, He said ... "My Son. For more than 50 years I have waited for you"…. As the message developed in my mind, tears began to stream down my face. He said, "My Son, I have tried every way that I could, to reach you,… for more than 50 years. But you closed yourself off to me and the entire world. I took this opportunity and used a man you have never spoken to or seen …. A total stranger ….to carry this message. I NEVER abandoned you, never betrayed you. I "Shadowed" you through all the years of your life …… your loneliness was my loneliness and your pain my pain, but you closed your heart to me." As all the blasphemies, profanities and cries of anger towards Him were replayed through the walls of my mind…… I threw my head down on my desk and I cried… openly! I cried in shame for what I had done to my God, to those who cared for me and to myself. Years of hate, torment and suffering. Years of drugs, alcohol, suicides and hospitals. As I sat there in shame and disbelief ….. I realized that there was a "Calling" on my life. A calling to share my experiences. I came to realize that God had planted Angels all through my life to guide me through my battles and when their job was done … He called them back home. I have never believed that God could have planned my life from Birth. But I realize now that all this was part of His plan and it must be shared for those who are just like me! Book one is titled. "The Journey". Book two is titled…. "The Calling".

Book One
The Journey

This is the story of a boy with a love for life, God and country that words cannot describe. A boy whose Hollywood fantasies ended with the realization of the brutalities of war. It's about the transformation that resulted in knowing that he had become what he hated most. A boy who waged a war against God that lasted more than forty years. Who turned away from all that he had been raised to believe and all those that loved him? It's about his struggles with depression and addictions, that within the walls of his mind, transported him into other worlds. It's about the never-ending mercies and love of God who shadowed him at every step that finally brought him back to life.

This book is dedicated to my wife, my mom and dad, and my sisters who loved me unconditionally throughout my ordeals. To my children and stepchildren whom I failed miserably, as a father. Know that I have always loved you. May this help you understand and forgive me. It's for all of America's soldiers who come home with battle scars, both mental and physical. Understand that a soldier is always a soldier, only the enemy changes. You must fight for life here, with the same determination and dedication as in any war zone in the world. Remember that life is precious, no matter what the circumstances. You must push forward to win each battle. Remember that life is a war with many battles. It's not important to win all the battles, it is important to win the war! Don't quit, don't give up! this is for all the addicts. May you know that the best is still ahead of you never behind you. Know that God loves you. Learn to love yourself and know how important you are. My addiction was all about me. About satisfying myself. There was no room for anyone else. Change that and you change your life!

It's for my grandbabies who have given their Pawpaw joy an old man never thought possible, It's for My God, who suffered the blame for all my mistakes and never stopped loving me or left my side. For all of you who know me and those of you who don't....... I thank you!

The Good Times

As I think back on my childhood, I recall the best years of my life. I remember being filled with good feelings. Feelings of love, joy and belonging.

I spent a lot of time watching TV, with westerns and war movies being my favorites. I used to get so wrapped up in the movies that I'd catch myself swaying from side to side as if I was actually dodging the bullets or arrows. When I saw "The Duke" put the grenades up to his mouth and pull the pin with his teeth I could almost taste the metal in my mouth. I fantasized of the glory and the feelings of being a good guy and fighting for what is right. Their battles were always for God, country and their way of life. Even as a child I grew up with a deep love for my country and our way of life. The National Anthem always sent chills up my spine. I led a very active life and fishing was my first love. There was just nothing that seemed to compare to being by the creek bed with my line in the water. My cousin Larry was my best friend and fishing buddy. (I realize today that he was also one of my Angels) We talked about everything. He was the brother I never had, and I loved him with all that was within me. We loved to be at our fishing hole laying back on the green grass, watching the white clouds roll by and talking about nothing that really mattered. Academically I did very well. I was on the honor roll every semester in elementary school. My grades only began to suffer when I found out the joys of being with the opposite sex. There was a railroad track by my house where I spent a lot of my time going thru rocks for my rock collection.

In the winter, when the days were cool and a brisk wind blew, I would go to the tracks, find a place where the grass was the tallest and lay there watching the clouds roll by. The grass would block the wind and I'd lay there, warm, happy and very much at peace. Church was always a big part of my life as a child. I was in all the Christmas and Easter plays and it seems like I was always memorizing something to recite in front of the congregation. The only problem there was that the call of the wild was often more than I could stand and sometimes got me into trouble. There was a river that ran by, close to the church and at times, when we were supposed to be in Bible class, we were out by the river throwing rocks at pigeons or skipping rocks across the water. When it was about time for Bible class to be over, we would wonder back to church and were often met by someone waiting at the door for us. It was real hard trying to make someone believe you were in Bible class when the bottom of your britches is wet, and your shoes are full of mud. Our family life was good. My three sisters and I got along well and me being the oldest, had to help take care of them. We ate as a family, vacationed as a family and went on Sunday drives as a family. I spent a lot of time taking things apart to see how they worked, and I had a deep hunger for knowledge. I had my nose buried in my encyclopedias a lot and spent hours with my chemistry set. I guess of all the people that I have met in my life, my Dad was my hero. He was the man that I knew I never could be. To me he was a very special man, very controlled, very sure of himself and very hard and efficient worker. I really don't think there was anyone else quite like him. The joy and peace in my life were at a maximum until Jr. high. There I found woman and a few bad habits. I remained popular and had my share of friends, but I found a new love, "Music" so I joined a band

and dropped to a "c" average. I still went fishing and was still active in church, but my heart was in music. When we would have band practice the girls would gather and you could almost take your pick. I also started smoking which was what I meant by "Bad habits. But I had also begun to run with a bad crowd and found myself doing things that were really disturbing to the "Church Side" of my learning. By the time I got to High school we were going on weekend tours that our band manager, set up, and I was eating up the life of a musician. The girls were plentiful, we were invited to all the parties and I considered myself very blessed. But the struggles with right and wrong became almost constant. My friendships were more challenging and my "heroes" changed from the good guys to the bad guys. In High school my troubles really started, I was so wrapped up in women, music and trouble that my grades took a nosedive. So finally, after very little deliberation, I decided to be a "Rock Star" and quit school. I thought my parents would shoot me, but they let me make my own decisions. Well, being a "Rock Star" wasn't all that great. While everyone else was in school I was on the street, alone, and it got really boring. The "Thugs" became my companions, as they were always around. Finally, one month after my seventeenth birthday I decided that since there was no war going on it would be a good time to join the Army, see the world and see what women from other countries looked like. I was also getting in a great deal of trouble. So, I went and talked to a recruiter and since my Dad had been in the Army, I went to the Army too. Being underage, the recruiter had to get my parents' signature, so we headed for the house. At the house we went over all the benefits, which were really good. He asked what I wanted to be, which at that time, I didn't know. My Dad had been a paratrooper, so he asked me if I had considered that. I told him I wasn't about to jump out of a perfectly good airplane and maybe not even a bad one and with all that settled they signed, and I was Government Issue. I automatically went back in my mind to the movies I had seen on TV and I knew well what a man in uniform does to women, I knew that I was going to love it.

Boot Camp

My first week in Basic Training is pretty vague, but I do know that Ft. Polk, Louisiana is not a good place to spend the winter. Most of us were very young and very homesick and the hours we kept were as bad as the food. We had a little runt for a Drill Sargent whose hook nose covered most of his face. He was short, thin and had a very rough voice that went very well with his personality. I often wondered, who had done what to him, to make him so mean, surely, he wasn't born that way. But I figured that maybe he had a really bad marriage and that's why he was so mean. I was pretty sure then, that I wasn't going to like Military life or him either! I adapted well, however, and as time went on, I could almost feel my body growing into the man that I wanted to be. We marched, played war games and at the sight of the flag I was still engulfed with chills of pride and love that I had for my country. By the time our last few weeks rolled around I was feeling almost like a man. I could drink almost as much beer as the rest of them and I didn't dislike my Drill Sargent quite as much as before. On Graduation Day we dressed in our Class "A" uniforms, marched out on the parade field and I felt sure of myself and very much at ease. It was a beautiful day. The sky seemed bluer than I had ever seen it before. My thoughts shot back to my railroad track, then to my cousin and our fishing hole. When the Drill Sargent got up on the platform to talk to us, he addressed us as "Men" and blew my mind. He even choked up a couple of times and I realized that he might be human after all. He told of of a conflict that was brewing somewhere in the middle east and he knew some of us would soon see combat. He explained that he was trying to prepare us for that and that is why he was so hard on us. I thought I saw his eyes watering up but maybe I was seeing things. I was glad to leave boot camp and was headed home for two weeks leave. I was ready for those women to fall at my feet in my uniform, at least that's the way the movies said it was supposed to be. So, I went to the airport, took a plane home and then took a cab to the house. My mother met me at the door and gave me a big hug which made me flash to a TV commercial that I had once seen. I kept my uniform on all the time that I was home, since my civilian clothes were fitting a little tight. I had filled out some at boot camp, but the real reason was that I still had my boot camp haircut which doesn't look good unless you're in uniform and then it still doesn't look good.

Well, my orders were for Ft. Ord, California which I was more than ready for. I had heard a lot about those "Wild" California women. But much to my disappointment, my wild time turned into a whole lot of work. I was in radio school and had to learn Morse code. Every time I thought that I had it down pat they would speed it up on me and I would fall behind again. They then took the top ten in the class and sent us to radio teletype school in Ft. Gordon, Georgia where we had to get a security clearance in order to stay in the class. We were told that upon completion of the school we would probably be assigned to a US Embassy overseas in some foreign country. I immediately pictured myself in a castle like building, leading the good life, sitting by a pool at night, sipping on a Martini as I chatted with some voluptuous female.

While I was there, I also came into contact with some paratroopers from the 82nd Airborne Division. They were wearing the same impressive uniform that the recruiter had shown me when he and my father were trying to get me to go Airborne except that they looked even better in person. Their uniforms were so heavily starched that I wondered if they bent their legs when they walked. Their jump boots were spit shined to the max. They wore a set of wings on their chest and a patch on their cap and shoulder that said "Airborne". I always stared so hard that I know they must have wondered if I wasn't "funny" or something. Sometimes at night I even dreamed about them, I had to have that uniform. I didn't really want to jump out of an airplane. I got dizzy just going up three stories. But I finally decided that I needed to overcome my fear of heights and go Airborne so I went and signed up hoping that when it came time for me to jump someone would push me out.

In the meantime, my top-secret clearance was denied, and I saw my dream castle crumble, the pool went dry and the voluptuous chic-split. I was being sent to Ft. Leonard wood, Missouri to be a combat engineer. I hated it! Towards the last few weeks, we got into the firing of different weapons, land mines, and explosives, this part I liked but the rest was the pits. I mean I couldn't picture my son someday coming up to me and asking what I did in the Army and having to tell him that I was a pontoon bridge builder. But by the end of the training, I received orders to go to Ft. Benning, Georgia for Airborne School.

Jump School

On arrival there we were given an orientation in which they stated that over half of us would drop out and not make it and I wondered what I had gotten myself into. The things we were expected to do were beyond belief. There were Marines and Air Force personnel there with us. I thought that I was in good shape after basic training but every morning I got up with muscles aching. I hurt in places I didn't even know that I had muscles. I spent most of my time there in the prone position knocking out push-ups but after a lot of vigorous training we were ready for our first jump. Well, I wasn't really ready for it, but they didn't ask me if I was. The plane was super noisy, and I was sitting there looking at the serious expressions on everyone's face that was sitting across from me. If I hadn't been so scared, I would have laughed. I wondered if they were thinking what I was thinking, "Will I freeze at the door," or "will my chute open?" My heart was beating so fast and hard that I wondered if the guys on either side of me could hear it. It seemed as though we flew around forever. Finally, we got word to stand up, hook up, and shuffle to the door. I heard the roar of the wind as they opened the door. I thought to myself, "Why are we even worrying about our chutes opening, when we step out that door the blast from the wind will probably kill us." I felt sick. That wind sure was making a lot of noise. For some reason I had sort of pictured the plane kind of parking until we were all thru jumping out. Word came to stand in the door, and I watched as the red light turned green. I heard the slap on the ass and the jump master yell "Go". Everyone started screaming "Go, go, go" and I knew good and well that nobody really wanted to go but we all went anyway. The next thing I knew I was looking at the outside of the plane, the ground then the sky then the plane again. I then felt a jerk that I thought would rip my legs off. I looked up, saw my chute was open and I thanked God. The first thing I did when I got back to the barracks was called my Dad and tell him that I had done it; He was very proud of me and I was very proud of me too. We were all in our barracks talking about the jump when the Sarge came in and asked us how we liked it "It was great Sarge, nothing to it," we said, "that's good cause you'll do it again tomorrow morning." I felt sick again! On graduation day our wings were pinned on our chest by a General and I felt that there was nothing in this world that I couldn't do I even had several dreams that I could fly, Yea - without a plane. I felt great. Not only was I wearing my dream uniform, but I was going to the same outfit where my Dad had been, the 82nd Airborne Division in Ft. Bragg North Carolina. Only one thing worried me. I had read in the paper that there was a revolution in the Dominican Republic and that they had sent the 82nd Airborne down there. I wasn't quite ready to go overseas yet, I mean, I hadn't even tried my uniform out on the women yet. Well, they didn't care and guess where they sent me? On the flight over I did a lot of thinking. I really wasn't ready to go overseas but at the same time my mind drifted in and out of movies that I had seen. I didn't think that it would be easy, but the end result would be worth it. I could already see the Welcome Home Parade with ticker tape and confetti falling like rain, me marching down main street with a chest full of medals and the girl that runs out of the crowd, throws her arms around me, kisses me, we get married and live happily ever after. Well, the fighting wasn't bad. The only thing that bothered me was that they spoke Spanish, my native tongue, and they kept yelling "Yankee Go Home" which made me feel unwanted. Soon all the fighting subsided, and we spent our weekends on the beach, drinking Dominican rum, eating pizza and loving their women. By this time the Viet-Nam war was making some of the headlines. We knew we wouldn't have to go because we were already serving a combat tour, but it was affecting our friends and relatives. I got word from home that my cousin Larry, my old fishing buddy, had joined the Marines and had orders to go to the Nam and this greatly upset me. He had always been my best friend and we had always shared everything. I started having dreams about him and he was always on my mind. I wanted to be with him, so I put in a request for a tour of duty in Viet Nam. About three months later they brought us back to the states. Then a few months later I received my orders for Viet Nam, so I was on my way home for two weeks leave before going to war again. My leave was a very emotional one with a lot of crying and carrying on. I expected that cause that's the way it was on TV I went to go say good-bye to my cousin Larry who had just returned from Viet Nam. I wondered as to where I had gone wrong since this just didn't work out the way it was supposed to. He was already back, and I was just going. I didn't want to go now, but again, nobody asked me. Anyway, I went to go see him and he got emotional. I had only seen this guy cry once in my life and this really worried me. He told me to keep my eyes open and keep my ass down and with that we parted company. We headed for the airport and I silently asked God to make me strong and not to let me cry and He did. Of course, everyone else cried but that was expected because that's the way the movies said it is supposed to be. My emotions were actually ripping me apart, but I fought to maintain. I kept visualizing bits and pieces of movies that I had seen. I knew this would be the real test of my manhood, but I again visualized the ticker tape parade when I got home, and I knew it would be well worth it. I didn't get my parade last time but then that wasn't a real war but when I come home this time it will all come to pass cause the movies said it would.

Headed to War

I was headed for Ft. Lewis Washington for two weeks and then on to Viet Nam. The feeling at Ft. Lewis reminded me of my first jump. Everyone was very quiet and very serious. It rained constantly and the fog and cloudy weather just added to our depressed state of mind. Then I figured out why they sent us here first. After two weeks here you almost want to get to Viet Nam just to see the sun again. The plane ride over was a little better. A few of us talked and I found some other guys that were going to the 101st Airborne which was where I was going. We arrived at Cam Ranh Bay with everyone very tense and the sign that told us what to do in case of a mortar attack didn't help any. But there was no mortar attack, and it was a beautiful day, so my mind drifted back to our old fishing hole and my days as a child and I longed to be there again. We had several orientations and then were sent to our separate units. I was going to Phan Rang which was my unit's base camp.

As we approached the camp, I noticed it looked deserted. I found out that everyone was out on an operation and we prepared for more orientations. During the orientation we could hear firing in the distance, and it was giving us the jitters. My mind drifted home and I wondered if I would ever see anyone again and what it was going to be like living in the jungle. We got a week of training in land mines and booby traps and that was all right because it was all sand and easy digging. It reminded me of "The Sands of Iwo Jima" with John Wayne. For a couple of days, it was just like in the movies and then the problems began. I couldn't find any grenades that I could pull the pin out with my teeth. Most of these were rusty and it took two hands to pull that pin out. The next thing was, they took me from my sandy by the beach paradise and sent me to my unit which was in a place called Khan-tum, a mountainous jungle crawling with slimy leeches, scorpions and centipedes. I couldn't for the life of me remember seeing this in the movies. Soon after that, people were shooting at me, not just shooting, but shooting at me in particular. I started not to like this movie. But I believed in what I was doing. I was a soldier and the love in my beliefs and my country grew even stronger. So, the "duke" didn't tell the whole truth, no big deal. In Khan-tum I was introduced to all the guys, handed a backpack and told to pack for a two-month operation. This was the "scruffiest" dirtiest bunch of guys I had ever seen. They were unshaven and filthy. Some of their pants were rotted and the inside seam had come apart making them look like dresses. They all had something written on their helmets, like, "Cong Killer", Born to Kill, "Ace" …. Except for one oddball, who had "God Walks With Me ", written on his. I found out later, his name was Woody. (I know today that Woody was one of my Angels). I didn't realize how small those packs were until I started to pack, I was neatly folding my socks, underwear, some foot powder, my toothbrush and trying to make the best of it but I didn't have enough room. I felt that I was being watched but every time I turned around, I saw no one watching me. I finally finished and that pack was bulging. Then here comes this guy with cases of C. Rations and I stood there looking at my backpack and the C rations. Again, I felt eyes on me, and I turned around and the guys were standing there laughing at me. I didn't think it was very funny and felt really stupid because I hadn't thought to leave room for any food. Woody came over and offered to help. He took my ruck sack, turned it upside down and dumped it. They laughed and said that I would need to pack a little food as we never know when our next resupply was going to be, and we couldn't be stopping by McDonalds every time I got hungry. I did think that was funny, so we all laughed. They packed my ruck sack with all the good rations that they thought I'd like, threw in some extra clips of ammo, extra grenades and eight canteens of water. The pack that earlier had looked so small now looked gigantic and I wondered if and how I was going to be able to carry it. I asked about an extra change of clothes and they laughed, this worried me. I was told that when the clothes I was wearing rotted off, I would get more, providing we could get some choppers to bring them out. I thought that was funny and I laughed ..... but they didn't.

The beautiful day began to darken as the sun set and as darkness grew my spirit also seemed to darken. I thought of home, of my folks and my sisters, and of all the good times with my cousin and our fishing holes. I asked God to help and strengthen me, that someday I may leave this place just as I came, and I believed that He would. We were going out on an operation the next morning, so I didn't get much sleep that night. It seemed as though I had just dozed off when it was time to get up. We ate quickly and started checking our weapons. We got more ammo pouches and more grenades, then word came to saddle up. I tried to heave the ruck sack up on my back, but I couldn't. Woody came over and told me to sit on the ground, put my arms thru the straps, roll over on my knees and then stand up. I did this and then followed everyone else to the waiting choppers. As I walked, I prayed to God for help.

Our first assault met no resistance. For several days we made no contact with the enemy at all and I thanked God. Then we got word over the radio that "A" Company had been hit hard and we were asked to assist. They were about a two day "hump" away from us if we walked day and night, so we did. We walked over boulders, around boulders, and thru boulders. Sometimes the openings between them were so small that we'd have to pull our packs off, crawl thru and then pull our packs thru.

When we contacted "A" Company on the radio we could hear very intense firing in the background. We knew that they needed help badly, so we walked day and night nonstop. I couldn't get over the total darkness of the jungle at night. It was like walking with your eyes closed. I was waiting to get my throat cut at any time. We would walk for a few yards, stop and whistle quietly, to guide the next man to you. He in turn did the same.

Finally, about noon of the second day we began to hear gunfire in the distance, and we knew we were close. A thousand things began to run thru my mind but at this point in time we were all too tired to worry much about the impending battle.

As we drew closer, we started drawing enemy fire from up above us. I heard a couple of rounds whistle past my ear, saw a couple of leaves fall from the camouflage in my helmet and I knew someone had me in their sites. I dropped and hit reverse, belly crawling backwards for about twenty feet. I heard the constant "Thud" of enemy grenades as they hit the ground and then the explosions that followed. I strained my eyes to catch sight of the enemy, but I saw nothing through the dense jungle. I looked around me for some of the guys and there was no one. I suddenly felt very alone and afraid as the gun fire and explosions became deafening. Then I heard screams for the Medic, and I knew I wasn't alone, but I also knew someone had been hit. I heard someone approaching and heard my name called. It was the guys who I was very glad to see. They told me we were going to start moving up the mountain, that part, I could have lived without. So, we started moving up, firing into the thick jungle growth and then suddenly it was totally silent, and the enemy was gone. We moved back and headed for "A" Company again. When we got there, it was unbelievable. As I walked down the path, my head moved from side to side looking at all the bodies lying on either side of the trail. There was moaning and crying, and little did I know that my movie was about to come to an end.

We couldn't medivac them from where we were because it was on the side of a very steep mountain. We had to take them to the base of the mountain to medivac. We all got bodies to carry and started moving down the side of the mountain. As darkness closed in around us the reality of where I was and what I was doing began to sink in.

The body that I was carrying was that of a black brother who had a hole above his left eye and another through his left lung. The mountain was so steep that we had to hold on to the trees with one hand and the, makeshift litter, with the other, trying to keep from sliding down the side. We often lost our footing and had to grab hold of a tree with both hands sending the body rolling down the side, stopping only when it slammed up against a tree with a sickening

"Thud". We retreated the body repeatedly, having to feel of the cold flesh and listen to the blood gurgling through the hole in his lung every time we moved his arm. At times the moonlight would shine through the trees and I could see his face. I found myself wondering about his family and how they would feel. I wondered if someday someone would be looking down on me thinking the same thing as they carried me to my last chopper ride. I found my thoughts flashing back to our living room. I visualized my sisters sitting there watching TV. I was home sick, and my insides ached for the touch of my mother and father. I needed to hear their voices telling me it would be alright. The movie ended as the pain of reality set in. Somehow that night we reached a place where we would try and get a med-vac in. This remains very clear in my mind. There were many trees, but their limbs had no leaves. The moon shown thru branches, casting Erie shadows across the ground. We laid our bodies down and watched as the rest of the guys dragged in carrying their dead and wounded. I looked around and there were bodies everywhere. There was crying and moaning, and, in my mind, the shadows of the dead trees seemed to be reaching out to me, to die as they had died. I grew very frightened and I wondered if I wasn't already dead and in hell. I felt like crying as I fought to regain control of my senses. I tried to remind myself that we hadn't slept or eaten for two days. I was shaking badly. I prayed and as I prayed, I wondered how many of them had also prayed to their God, only to have been forsaken. I remembered a story I had heard as a child about a man called Job and how he threw his arms up and asked God why He had forsaken him. As I stood there shaking, I looked up thru the trees, at the heavens and I knew God was up there somewhere. I had an emotional

battle raging within me. I thought of my parents and sisters and longed to be home like never before. My heart was heavy with pain and my emotions raged but no tears fell. That night I begged God not to let me die in this nightmare and from somewhere came some relief and I felt safe. Shortly after that we heard the familiar sound of choppers coming and we evacuated the dead and wounded. I opened up a can of cookies and I ate. We saddled up and moved to a nearby hill, dug our foxholes as I lit a small fire to warm my food, I heard a voice …. It was "Wierdo" (Woody) coming to share food with me. As we ate, he pulled out his little Bible and read. Soon after, we were asleep. When we awoke the next morning, we ate quickly and were off again to where we had been before. To pursue and, if possible, annihilate the enemy. We met little resistance and I was having a great deal of trouble with the memories from the night before. My shoulders were bleeding from where the straps from the ruck sac had rubbed them raw. We came to a very swampy area on the other side of the mountain. It was very hot, and my shoulders ached from the weight of the ruck sac. We were extremely tired. We were walking thru ankle deep water and I could see the leeches circling my boots. This grossed me out knowing they were after my blood. I saw a black man fall out about twenty feet in front of me. He just collapsed face down in the filthy water. We stopped momentarily while the sarge came back and took a look at him. I bent over at the waist to take some weight of my shoulders. I watched as the sarge told him repeatedly to get up. Then he said to move out and if he didn't get up, to leave him. I walked around him and felt sorry for him because I knew how he felt. I kept looking back and I saw him get up and start walking. I was relieved. I was in a great deal of pain, but I would stop when everyone else stopped. That night we made camp by a stream bed. I was beat and my shoulders were killing me. I couldn't stand to wear my shirt as it rubbed against my raw shoulders, so I took it off. Soon I was asleep. About an hour later I awoke in great pain. I ran my hand across my chest, and I felt slimy lumps all over me. I jumped up in horror. Someone came over and sprayed alcohol all over my chest and the leeches fell off. I settled back down as I cussed the leeches. I woke up the next morning with my shoulders still hurting. I sat up and looked around. The smell of alcohol was strong as everyone was spraying their area for leeches. I looked at the ground around me and it was covered with worm like creatures. They would stand straight on end, very still, and as soon as you moved, they would crawl towards you. This was really gross. We moved out into a very thick jungle. I was amazed at how dark the jungle could be in broad daylight. The vegetation was magnificent. The air smelled fresh as it does after a spring rain. Some of the insects looked like flowers. This took me back to the Tarzan movies I had seen on TV, all except the leeches. We stopped for a break along the trail and I slipped the straps off of my raw shoulders. My weapon lay across my lap, my finger on the automatic fire lever. Suddenly I Heard a rustling to my right. I got to my feet, squatting and facing the direction of the sound, ready to flip to auto fire. Whatever it was, it was headed my direction. My heart pounded with anticipation. I would soon have my first body count. The brush next to me moved and I stepped back ready to open up. Then this big orange head worked its way out followed by a lot of green legs. It looked like a giant centipede about two feet long. I wasn't sure what to do. One of the guys came over and killed it with the butt of his weapon. I said nothing, just stood there looking dumb.

We moved all day, and I thanked God we had made no contact. I was kind of enjoying this stroll thru what I imagined the garden of Eden must have been like. We humped another five hours and stopped again. I was pulling drag (the last man in the column), so I sat looking back to make sure no one sneaked up on us. My mind flashed back to the Tarzan movies. I had always wondered what it would be like to be in a jungle and now I was there.

My First Kill

Suddenly, I spotted movement. I rose slowly to my feet, not moving my eyes off the target. I knew this had to be Charlie. My heart raced. There was no place to hide and I couldn't see much thru the thick jungle. Again, I saw movement and thru a small clearing I spotted black pajamas. It was Charlie. I flipped my weapon to auto and fired off a burst of rounds. Whatever it was fell. I went over to check my first body count, feeling more like one of the guys now, with my first body count. I approached cautiously, keeping my weapon at the ready. I looked down, and in disbelief uttered "God no". I felt sick and in pain. There was my body count. A woman dressed in black pajamas. In one hand she clutched an American Bible, and she was unarmed. She laid there looking up at me, moaning. I said" My God what have I down?" I felt totally helpless. I was sorry. I wanted to fall to my knees and cry out for forgiveness, but I didn't. I felt a hand on my shoulder, and someone said, "There's nothing we can do for her but put her out of her misery." An M79 was placed under her chin, and with a roar, the top of her head was gone. We saddled up and moved on. A little way up the trail we found her hooch (house) and we burned it. I tried to block her from my mind but her pleading eyes and her moaning haunted me. I had my first body count, and like the guys say, "It isn't nothing but a thing."

We moved until almost dark and found a place to set up for the night. I was tired and sore as I began digging my foxhole. The women's eyes darted in and out of my mind and I wanted to go home. I felt like a child and I needed my mother and father to tell me not to be afraid, everything would be all right. I felt so alone. I hurt miserably and I wondered what I would be like if I lived long enough to leave this hell. As I wallowed in my sorrow, I heard a gentle voice, almost in a whisper say, "Are you all right?" For a minute I thought it was God. I turned and it was the strange young man with God walks with me written on his helmet. We talked for a while and he told me his name was Woody. He carried a small bible with him and as we shared our meal he read. It seemed a little awkward, but I would find this young man and his Bible every night at my campfire as he shared God with me. I needed this young black man and I thanked God for him. The black of the night is indescribable. You sit as though your eyes are closed and your mind begins to play tricks on you. I kept imagining the muzzle of a rifle pointed straight at my head as I waited for the pull of the trigger. I would reach out to grab it but there was nothing there. To read our watch we caught light bugs and put them in a medicine bottle and when we needed to see the time, we shook it, and they would light up so we could read our watch. To wear a luminous watch was sure death.

By now, our food and water were running low and our clothes were beginning to rot. We needed a resupply which meant that we would also get mail from home. I longed to read words from home. My mind needed a rest from this hell; and little did I know that this was only the beginning. The next morning, we ate quickly, covered up our foxholes and moved out. We moved for several hours when I heard gun fire from the front of the column. I heard a simultaneous click as our weapons went on full auto. Our senses were on full alert. More fire broke out and word came back to drop our packs and move forward. We ran up the path jumping over back packs. We came to a clearing and stopped. What was up ahead appeared to be a VC basecamp. We started drawing incoming fire and we scrambled for cover. We were told to spread out and rush the camp. We spread and came out of the jungle at a dead run, jumping over several enemy bodies as we advanced. We had them on the run and reacted much as wild animals do at the smell of blood. They seemed to disappear as quickly as they appeared, running into the cover of the jungle. I hated going back into the jungle, but we were following a blood trail and that's where it led us. As we entered the jungle, I turned and saw the last of one of our other squads entering to our left. We followed the trail as it weaved thru the jungle. I then heard our point man open up with automatic fire. As we peered thru the dense jungle, we could make out movement about fifty yards in front to our right. Suddenly incoming rounds began to hit all around us, and we dove for cover. The roar of our weapons was deafening, as we returned fire. I heard cries for medic and my insides turned as I wondered who had been hit. We heard cries of pain and more calls for medic, only it was coming from the direction that we were firing. Cries of "Cease fire" filled the air and the roar of weapons ceased. The cries and moans of wounded soldiers filled the air as we fought with our minds for an explanation. How could this be, how could God have allowed this? How could Charlie evade both squads and lead us into one another? We had shot our own men. I wondered if one of my bullets had brought down our men. I hated these people, while at the same time, I admired their war skills. As we carried our casualties back to the VC basecamp to be medevacked, I couldn't bear to look at them. I kept my eyes straight ahead as my emotions raged. What I felt inside me, towards God frightened me. We began searching the tunnels and set fire to everything else. I walked up to four VC who were taken prisoner. I watched as they interrogated them. I watched as their throats were slashed. Their bodies were placed against a fallen tree; their arms arranged around each other as if they were shooting the breeze. Cigarettes were placed in their mouths and our unit patch was tacked to their foreheads. We wanted them to know who had done the butchering. They looked rather humorous, in a sick sort of way. I wondered what it would feel like to cut someone's throat. I knew that, in the future, I would find out and this frightened me.

The Transformation

My feelings had begun to bother me. My mind fought with the laws of God. It was getting harder to distinguish right from wrong. I began to have spells of intense hate and anger and I begged God to make it stop. We set up an ambush that night, in case Charlie returned during the night. The darkness always tested my mind. It was easy to imagine so many things. It gave you so much time to think that sometimes it was more of a test than the actual battles. I thought of the men we had lost that day and I wondered when mine would come and how I would get mine. I looked up at the sky, the stars were bright and beautiful. A light mist had begun to fall, and the earth was sending up its natural scents. I listened to the sounds of the different animals that infested the jungle and my mind drifted back to the Tarzan movies. I smiled to myself, as I pictured our living room, my parents and my sisters. My insides ached as the desire for the world tore at me. I was a soldier now and I had to be strong and with this I tried to get some rest. The next morning, we called in choppers to transport confiscated enemy papers and weapons back to the rear. They brought us out clean pants and socks and our beloved mail. It was always good to hear from the world. As we read, we escaped this hell hole we were in. Letters reminded us of the reason we were here. Woody came over and we shared news from home and, of course, he read from his little Bible. Woody knew what I was going thru. He constantly searched my eyes as people do when they are searching your soul. He knew I was drifting away from God and I thanked God for my special friend. We got word to saddle up and get ready to move out. My ruck sac was full again. We never like running low on food and ammo but it sure does feel better toting a half full ruck sac than a full one. We began to move out, the ruck sac digging into my shoulders again. We were on another winding trail and I wondered what the enemy had against straight trails thru the jungle. We followed this trail for two days with no contact. I was glad not only for the physical part of it, but it gave our minds time to heal. We came to the edge of the jungle and stopped. There was a rice paddy stretching across a valley with a large village in the center. We would move across and take the village. I didn't like having to cross such a large open area with no cover if we got hit. We moved quickly to take the villagers by surprise. It was hard to surprise Charlie. He always knew where we were. Every night we dug foxholes and all he had to do was follow the foxholes. Our fire power was unmatched, so he was never anxious for a direct confrontation. We were on the dykes of the rice paddies when all hell broke loose. We had no cover, so we had to drop into the filthy waters of the rice paddies for cover. The water leeches moved in quickly. Water leeches aren't like land leeches and are much bigger. The firing was more intense than I ever heard before and I heard screams for the medic. We couldn't move and were pinned down by the intense fire. I heard the CO radio for assistance; I could tell from the look on his face that he didn't like the response. We had to move, so we began to crawl over the dike and dropped into the water on the other side. We crawled neck deep in the filthy water with the leeches circling. I felt stings on my legs, and I knew lunch was being served. I flashed back to the movies and I couldn't remember the Duke ever having this problem. We crawled until we reached another dyke, stopped and returned fire. My weapon was over heating and began to jam. I heard the CO yelling at someone on the radio telling them to come in and it didn't matter how close we were. I had a feeling I knew what he was saying, and I wish he would have consulted me before getting me killed, but he didn't. I thought he had called in artillery support but when I heard the roar of jet engines, I knew I was wrong. I looked to the sky and saw them approaching already in a dive and I knew the guns would soon follow. We bolted straight up and ran the other direction as fast as our little legs would carry us. I heard the guns open up, bombs exploding but never looked back, just kept running. When we were far enough away, we stopped and watched. It was great. Those fly boys put on a show. The jets tore up that village and the old prop planes came in with napalm and set everything on fire. I saw America's fire power firsthand. We moved in and took what was left of the village. People came from everywhere. There were men, women and children bleeding and moaning as smoke filled the air and the fires raged. Burning bamboo popped and smoke filled the air. We took 185 prisoners and as darkness fell, we formed a human chain around them. This was my first chance to observe these animals we were at war with. I watched, my eyes feeding on every move they made. I hated them; they were ugly people. I watched their eyes as they walked by me, my finger tightening on the trigger. They would look at me as though searching my eyes and then look away. I could see the hate and fear in their eyes. As I watched I thought of the men we had lost, and the words of my mind screamed at them to attack me so I would have reason to shoot them dead. I wanted them to hate me. I looked in the eyes of the children and saw fear. I searched their eyes for hate but found none and it angered me; I wanted them to hate me so I could hate them back. They needed to hate me to make this right. I grew afraid and I asked God to restore my sanity. My battles with God had grown very heavy these days and it worried me. I watched them move as people and not animals. I saw the fear and understood it. I put myself in their place and felt compassion. This angered me, for these were animals and I had to hate them. The words of my mother and God's commandments haunted me. The pictures of my mind ran wild with men that I had seen die. I could see their eyes so clearly. The pleading eyes of the woman I killed darted in and out of my mind. I felt myself drifting away from God and at the same time felt as if I must, or I would lose my sanity and maybe my life. Although my thoughts of God were there, I realized I hadn't prayed in a long while. The thoughts of God were there because I couldn't escape them. They were bred into me. I no longer prayed because I had no right. The path that I had chosen was not of God, but I must follow it, so I continued the journey. The next day I awoke fairly refreshed. At least we didn't have to dig a foxhole this one night. Woody came over and told me to report to the CO. who wanted to know if I could boobytrap the bodies. I could use grenades hidden under their shirts and when they rolled them over it would set them off. I rolled the first body over and his brains poured out. The second one, my hand slipped into the hole in his chest. By the time I finished I had blood and guts all over me. I had begun to hate the smell of blood. It had such a strong, sweet kind of odor. The choppers came in to pick up the prisoners as we finished burning and killing all the animals. The guys were kidding me about what a soldier I had turned out to be because of all the blood stains on my clothes. In a way, I enjoyed It, as I wondered what God thought. There was an old Sarge, as we called him, and he came and told me not to let it bother me. They were kidding me because they liked me. We walked together for a while and he told me about himself. I had seen him before and found myself watching him at times. He was older and had grey hair. He was tall and always walked with a walking stick he had made from an old limb. He carried a sport section from some newspaper in the side pocket of his trousers and I noticed that he read it over and over. I wondered why someone that old would be out here with us. We had a good talk as we walked thru this valley and as he departed, he asked me to come eat with him. I did and we talked for a while. Yes, Woody was there with his little Bible. The old sarge got up to leave and he leaned over and said," Just remember, it ain't nothing but a thing. I said, "Yea, I know". When he disappeared, I wondered "What the hell did that mean?" But it was a good talk and I felt that God had sent him to help me get my head straight. The journey thru the valley was very peaceful. I figured we had raised so much hell that everyone packed up and left. I noticed we were headed towards a mountain range. I was glad because these valleys were really hot with not much shade. We stopped about an hour before sundown and I dug my foxhole in just a few minutes. I saw the old sarge coming and we ate together along with Woody, my usual companion, and we listened as Woody read. Darkness came quickly as we began to set our flares, mines and booby traps. The next morning, we ate and moved out to the mountain range. Word was that we were after a regiment of NVA, supposedly camped at the top of those mountains. In a couple of hours, we reached the base and started up the side. These were the highest mountains I had ever seen and the farther up we went, the steeper they got. On the second day we were climbing almost straight up. If the man in front of you wasn't careful, he would start rocks and dirt falling and hit you in the head. That night, instead of digging foxholes, we straddled trees to keep from sliding down the side. On the third day we reached the top and it was breath taking. I flashed back to the old Tarzan movies I had seen. The top was flat with shrubs and green grass that looked as if it had been mowed. You could look down into the village and see the clouds drift by. We walked along the top for three days and killed three VC. By the third day I was ready to get out of these mountains. It got downright cold at night and the wind blew constantly. It was hard to distinguish movement and sound with the wind blowing all the time, that was dangerous. We began to move down the other side of the mountain and it was also very steep. It was covered with elephant grass about eight feet tall. My trousers had rotted and come apart at the seams, looking much like a dress. As soon as you stepped on the elephant grass you slid down the mountain until you hit a tree. The edges of the elephant grass were sharp and cut you easily. We didn't wear underwear, so we were FULLY exposed, and our delicates were being butchered. Then when your sweat hit your delicates, it stung. We finally reached the bottom, where we found another village that we were ordered to search and destroy. We swept into this village undetected; there were no men, only women and children. We killed all the animals and burned all the hooch's except for one. There was a woman inside and she appeared to be in labor, so we left her alone. That night we set up camp overlooking the village. We hadn't had much action, so I didn't dig a very deep foxhole. I was pulling my turn on guard, totally engulfed by darkness, thinking about home, God and the pictures of my mind...... when I noticed that there was no sound. The usual night creatures were silent, and I knew something was wrong.

Something was fixing to come down. I was going to pass the word when I heard a series of "thuds" and about three of us yelled "grenades." I hit my foxhole and a series of explosions followed. I heard the shrapnel from the grenades zing by me. I laid back in my foxhole with no room for my legs. I heard the shrapnel hitting around me and prepared myself for pain and maybe death. I was so afraid; I pulled my ruck sac down on top of me and I waited to die. Then suddenly it stopped. I was blind. I could see nothing, and I reached for my weapon. Then all hell broke loose with automatic weapons fire. I could hear the bullets whistle by me as I sat in total darkness. I opened up with automatic weapons fire, screaming like a mad man, firing clip after clip until my weapon over heated and jammed. There was total silence. I wanted to yell out at somebody but couldn't until I knew who was out there. I sat in total darkness not knowing what to do and not knowing which direction I was facing. I wondered if anyone was alive. I heard movement and turned to fire when I heard English voices. I had lost my sense of direction and wasn't sure which way I was facing. I heard the old sarge and Woody talking, they were looking for me. I said I was all right and we searched for others. We had several dead and some wounded. In the morning we found several enemy dead and some wounded. All were women. One of them was the woman we had mercy on because we thought she was in labor. We called in choppers for our dead and wounded. One of the dead would have been home in less than a month. I questioned God and grew angry. My mind screamed at God while my heart cried, for I knew there was much more to come.

That night was very hard for me. The women's pleading eyes haunted me as I told myself repeatedly that this was part of war. I remembered the eyes of the children and the need that I felt to hate them. I remembered the body of the soldier that I carried for two days. I wanted to stop the pictures of my mind, but I didn't know how. I could no longer pray to God, for I was angry and ashamed. I thought of my family and friends back home. If they knew what I was doing they would hate me as I was growing to hate myself. I spoke to Woody and asked him how he could have God walks with me on his helmet, when everything we do is against God's commandments. I told him that I blame God for all the suffering and dying. He looked at me in his unmoving manner and said that God doesn't make wars, man does…. but God always gets the blame. I dissected his words and I fought with what he said. I didn't want to believe in God anymore, it was tearing me apart. How can you live killing and mutilating and still believe in God? I felt guilty, ashamed and afraid and at times I felt as though I hated God. The next morning, we moved out of the village. I turned and saw the woman who had deceived us hanging by her feet from a tree with her throat cut. I guess she committed suicide! We continued our sweep thru the valley and were now very tired and our clothes were beginning to rot. Some of us were developing jungle rot from the cuts of the elephant grass. We were out of food and began to ration. We had not had mail for quite some time now. This valley was extremely hot and for two more days we continued our sweep. The CO was getting desperate for a resupply. I heard him telling someone on the radio that we had to have a resupply within the next two days. He was told that all the choppers were busy supporting troops engaged in heavy combat and that we would have to hold on for a few more days. So, we spread a poncho on the ground, and we walked by dropping in what food we had left so we could split it up equally. All I had left were cans of peanut butter. As I walked by, I looked in to see what goodies everyone had thrown in. It looked as though we're going to be eating a lot of peanut butter cause that's all that was in there. We sent out a patrol to search for wild potatoes, pineapples or peppers but found nothing. I figured God was still upset with us because of the woman who committed suicide, but it isn't nothing but a thing. We found a creek nearby and washed our jungle rot for the first time in a long time. The old sarge, Woody and I went and jumped in and were quickly covered with leeches. We had just finished pulling them off when some more of the guys came. We let them get in and waited. They were having a really good time when one of them started shouting. They all headed for the shore but kept slipping on the moss-covered rocks and falling back in. We laughed at the site of their clumsy retreat. I realized that I hadn't laughed for a very long time, and it was good.

Woody

The next morning, we got up and waited for the choppers to come in so we could eat. Finally, we heard the familiar sound of chopper blades. We not only got mail, clean clothes, ammo and food but we got a hot meal. We got candy bars and a real treat. We got one hot beer each. We were in heaven. The hill we were on was like a small park, green grass and shade to lay around and enjoy our beer and mail. We sat and drank beer, read mail and enjoyed ourselves like we hadn't done in a really long time. My mother had sent me a magazine with pictures of all the new cars. We picked out the car we were going to get when we got back to the world. We left the war for a while and it was good. We finally began to move again. We were still enjoying the peace and beauty of this place when an explosion sounded towards the front of the column. We wondered who had gotten his. Was it a booby trap or land mine? I moved up slowly looking for booby traps or land mines. I wondered who had been hit. I glanced up at a big bolder and saw a pair of boots sticking out from the far side. I could tell that whoever it was on the far side was dead. I got closer and saw a helmet on the ground splattered with blood. My mind and body seemed to go into convulsions. On the helmet was written, "God walks with me." I screamed at God. "NOooo .....He loved you, how could you allow this?" I looked at the bloody face of my beloved friend and wept. I screamed but made no sound. I picked up his helmet and held it to my chest as my heart bled. I cussed God for the first time in my life. I hated Him.

I'm not sure how long I stood there. I don't even remember what happened for about the next three days. My insides bled for the loss of my dear friend. I seemed to have left, mentally. I would sometimes leave and come back again. The next thing I remember was being on choppers headed back to the rear for a four-day rest and out to the South China sea to soak in and heal our jungle rot. We spent the next four days eating real food, drinking beer, and swimming in the South China sea, but the thoughts of my dear friend were very present. What would I do without Woody?

I was glad when we loaded up on choppers and headed back to war. This was giving me too much time to think. I needed to be out in the jungle. I was now a war hardened squad leader and was always on the first chopper out so we could locate the mine fields and booby traps. It was a nice day as we flew out, our legs dangling out the side of the chopper. I looked at the choppers beside us and the gunships that escorted us and I felt an awesome power. I checked my weapon and grenades and my mind said, "This is where you bastards pay for Woody." I always prayed on my way to an assault, but I couldn't do that anymore. Suddenly the door gunner opened up and the gunships began sending a barrage of rockets and I was ready. Our chopper shot ahead of the others and started to descend. We were drawing small weapons fire as we jumped from the chopper. We dropped our packs and lobbed grenades into the tree line. I felt a sharp pain in my leg and had hit a punji stick which pierced my leg. I called for the rest of the company to come in and warned them of punji sticks as we cleared for land mines. We were using mine detectors to clear. We had a colonel coming in that evening to get with our CO on this operation and they wanted him to be safe. Word had it that this was an operation, with the Marines sweeping in from one side and the Big Red One from the other. So, we began to set up camp. I was sitting in my foxhole having my usual mental battles when I heard an explosion from the direction of the CP. I crawled up to the CP and found the colonel laying there dead, along with the CO and the first sarge had a butt full of shrapnel. I knew that, somehow, we had missed a land mine. I fought with myself all night, trying to figure out how this could have happened. We had covered all the ground except where we had dropped our ruck Saks. If there was a mine, the ruck Saks would have set it off, but the weight of the ruck Saks wasn't enough to set off the mine. It took a man's weight to set it off.

The next day we moved out and I volunteered for point. I spent all day blazing a trail, with a machete thru elephant grass eight feet high. We came up on a village and when I walked around to the front of the hooch, I found a man sitting there making punji sticks, like the one I got in my leg. He hadn't seen me yet, so I stood there and watched. He had a small boy helping him and I walked up so they could see me. He never raised his head but just looked at my boots then followed them up to my face. He smiled a sick smile and began to grab handfuls of punji sticks and breaking them. I smiled back and smashed his head with the butt of my rifle. The kid began screaming so I shut him up too. I moved on to another hooch and found a man and woman holding a baby in another hooch. The man put his hands together and began to bow at the waist in a sign of welcome. This was a VC village, and I knew it. I fired up the husband as his wife looked on. Then I dragged him out by the corral. I brought the woman out to see her husband. I watched to see her react, but she showed no emotion as she stood there with her baby. I grabbed him and threw him into the corral with the pigs. I watched her as she saw the pigs ripping the flesh off his body. she stood there doing nothing. I grew angry, I wanted her to scream and cry. I wanted her to hurt as I was hurting, and it made me furious. I flipped my weapon to automatic and they were gone. I killed the pigs, water buffaloes and everything else I saw. I stood and saw all I had done, and I thought of Woody. I jumped as I felt a hand on my shoulder. It was the old sarge. He asked if I was alright and I said yes. He said I didn't look like it and began to talk to me. He said he had been in the Korean War too. He said he had seen his brother killed there. He was almost in tears as he told me of the anger and pain and the GOD thing. I listened and I hurt for him. He said I reminded him of the way he was and told me that it would destroy me in spirit, if not in body unless I learned to control it. I knew what he was saying. I just didn't know how.

The next morning, we moved out. This was a very large valley called the A-shua Valley, along the Cambodian border. I didn't even like the sound of that. The sarge and I Spoke often but I found myself growing distant not really wanting to talk. We talked but things were changing for me. Every day was an emotional battle. That night we set up on a hill and dug our foxholes. They asked for volunteers for an ambush. I volunteered. We set up next to a village. We had been ordered not to use our weapons, just our knives. We didn't want to give away our position. We spread out and waited. We sat in the waters of a rice paddies and waited. I never liked being in these nasty waters that were always infested with leeches, but somehow, it just didn't matter anymore. After a few hours of darkness, the trail became heavily traveled. We each took a man, killed him, and hid the body. Something happened with one of the guys and I heard a shot ring out, which gave away our position. We immediately drew intense incoming fire, and we were greatly outnumbered. We radioed in for support and they sent us a plane called "Puff The magic dragon". I never saw so much fire power in a single aircraft. It was dark and we couldn't see the aircraft only the fire from its guns and it was awesome.

We moved back to our unit and moved into the village. We dropped our packs and moved in quickly. We were drawing small arms fire and Charlie was hitting those tunnels. I saw the old sarge move up beside me. I spotted a Charlie headed for a tunnel. The old sarge was pursuing another to my left and I saw him out of the corner of my eye. I saw the Charlie he was after hit a tunnel and he went in right after him. Everything seemed to shift into slow motion as I lost track of the one, I was after and replayed what the old sarge had done. My mind screamed "Noooo". I heard the explosion, saw the dust coming from the tunnel and I knew my old friend was dead. I ran to the tunnel, waited for the dust to settle and went in. I found his weapon and what was left of him. I said nothing as my soul screamed in agony. I thought of his family and all that he had shared with me. God, he was all that I had left. Why? I don't know what happened next. I seemed to have blacked out for some time. This was a very large tunnel complex and we called in experts to gas the tunnels. I was emotionally dead. I mourned my dear friend.

We went on with our sweep and moved into another village. It too, was filled with tunnels. I saw movement to my left as if someone had entered the tunnel. I approached the entrance and told them to come out, in Vietnamese. I grabbed a grenade and tossed it into the tunnel. After the dust settled, I entered. I found the remains of three little girls about eight years old. My mind flashed back to my sisters and I screamed to God. I grabbed one by the wrist to drag her out and her arm came off in my hand. I dropped to my knees and cried. Why God .... Why are you doing this to me? They ran out of fear and this animal came and destroyed them. But they were the enemy, they deserved to die. No, they were innocent children. God, let me die. Stop the suffering. I no longer worried about dying, only about living.

We set up that night overlooking a heavily traveled trail. Actually, it was quite beautiful, but I found it difficult to see beauty in anything anymore. The next morning, we were about to move out when we spotted two gooks coming up the trail. They stopped and appeared to be looking at something in the stream. I could feel the hate rise in me. I wanted to kill them now. The thought of them getting away was more than I could bare. They started towards us and we opened up and there were two less gooks to worry about. We went down to search them. One was still alive. I grabbed his hair, yanked his head back and with the stroke of my Bowie, he was gone. A little later a few more came along and it was a turkey shoot. We must have killed fifteen gooks and were running out of places to stash the bodies.

We decided that we had been there too long. To remain in one place was dangerous, so we moved. We headed back to the mountain range and the jungle. The jungle is a treacherous place, full of insects and animals. It's a struggle for life. The leeches, scorpions, snakes, centipedes and bees are all out to kill you. In order to survive you must become one of them. You must stop seeing life, only death. You stop seeing good, only evil. You stop feeling joy, only hate; so, you kill and destroy and your content because you have become a good soldier. But you have also become what you hated most. You're not even an equal, your worse. But you survive….. or have you died? Your thoughts of family and home have become a fairy tale. Your family is crawling around on the jungle floor, and you are filled with shame and hate.

We moved back into the valley with an assault on a village. We took three prisoners and the CO said to make them talk. I had been sent two new men to my squad and I told them to look and learn. I told them to watch the two prisoners and I took the other and tied him to a tree for target practice. He wouldn't talk and was dying, but he wasn't going to cheat me as I jerked his head back and introduced him to my Bowie. I walked back to the other prisoners and they began to talk to the interpreters. My men followed. One asked how long I had been in country and I said, "Too long." and walked off. In a way I wanted to speak to them. I could see the fear in their eyes. But I knew what it meant to get close to someone, even to know anything about them was not good. The less you know, the less you have to think about when they're lying there dead. With everyone that dies, you lose a part of yourself and before long there is nothing left of you to give. The memories that once brought you joy, seem distant and unreal. I didn't believe that I would ever see my mother, father and sisters again. You must except the fact that you are home and what you have become. This is where you belong. If civilization ever existed, you didn't belong there.

They say that if you make it thru your first 30 days your good….. until your last 30. I found this to be true more often than not. I have been here too long now. I was hard and tough and didn't like it. I could no longer believe there was a God and live the way I lived. There was an incredible battle raging within my soul and mind. I feared nothing and no one. The deep beliefs that I had arrived with, no longer existed. I had become God, for I decided whether you lived or died. I fought the mental flashes of home, love and family. My soul was totally engulfed with a cold penetrating pain that overwhelmed me with shame for what I had become. I felt that I could no longer leave this place. I played with the leeches that I had once found so repulsive. They had become my friends. I realize now that they only kill so that they may live, while I only lived so that I may kill. The lowest form of life no longer crawled around on the jungle floor, it walked upright as a man. It was me. I can't put into words the agonizing pain and shame that you feel when you have to turn loose of all that was love and good, for the realization that you are where you belong and have become what you hated most. From the depths of my soul, I cried out, pleaded and screamed condemnation to God but never shed a tear or uttered a word. Where I once worried about dying, I now worry about living. My movie ended with no good feelings, no good guys and no parade. All that was left was the reality of total destruction and death.

The next morning, we moved out on our usual search and destroy mission, sweeping across a valley, when one of our squads reported being pinned down by heavy automatic weapons fire. We had a new Co, code name "Zorba the Greek". I never paid a lot of attention to them because they normally, didn't last long. They carried a modified version of our M16 and Charlie new that only officers carried them. The first thing we told a new CO is, get rid of that weapon. Charlie always has snipers watching, they see that weapon and "Bang", your dead. This man was different. He always wanted to be in the action and never told us to do anything he himself wouldn't do. He called in gunships and they were soon circling the area answering with gun and rocket fire. Great job, Zorba!

One day we were crossing a rice paddy and drew intense fire from two sides. We called in gunships and soon they were circling the area. Zorba called for one of the gunships to pick him up so he could see from the air, what exactly we were up against. The gunship came in and picked Zorba up. They circled the area and came in for a landing. I watched Zorba as he readied to exit, then suddenly I saw him slump. They landed and as we rushed to Zorba's aid, I heard the familiar gurgling of blood as we moved him, and I knew death was at hand. I saw him die and could not force tears into my eyes for the rage within the walls of my mind, but the war raged on.

Our next assault was on a mountain top and it went well with little conflict. We were winding down the mountain when I heard fire from the front of the column. I was used to this as the adrenaline shot thru my views delicately wiring all my senses. Dirt was kicking up in front of me, so I knew someone had me in their sights as I crawled backwards. We fired into the dense jungle above, not being able to see thru the thick vegetation. Word came to me that the CO wanted me. There was a dry stream bed and when they tried to cross it, they were gunned down. Charlie had set up a machine gun covering that stream bed. We had a man lying in the stream bed with hits on both legs. Every time someone tried to assist, they were gunned down. I figured I could work my way up the stream bed and blow some trees across the bed so we could have some cover and then extract the wounded man. The man was screaming in pain and I saw a comrade run across the stream to assist and was gunned down. They began rolling his body down the stream bed, with gun fire, leaving a trail of grey brain matter and intestines strung down the stream bed. His wounded comrade was still screaming, calling on God and begging for help. Suddenly, there was an explosion, and he was silent. I never knew what exactly happened that day...... and I never asked! I continued in my quest for revenge. Somehow, I believed that the killing would ease the pain, that if I killed enough it would go away. They say that you should not look at the face of someone you kill. They say that the face will haunt you. But I wanted to see their faces. I wanted to see the fear but most of all I wanted to see the pain. I wanted to see them wrench in agony and cry out for mercy .... but they never did.

Much of what followed is unclear as I began to drift in and out of reality. Maybe God took mercy on me, I don't know. I knew I was where I belonged. I knew I could no longer hate the enemy without hating myself. The pain and hate totally engulfed me as I waged war on a God I once loved. I was dead and my body shut down. I don't remember going home. I later asked my mother how I got home, where I came in at and how did I get to the house. I was back in the world now, but the war raged on.

The Home Coming

I left the war on the verge of insanity. Everything I had been raised to believe died in the jungles of Vietnam. As a person subjected to great pain, deliriously goes in and out of consciousness, so was I, from one state to another, from one world to another.

Shortly after coming home, I was married. I was introduced to her before the war, so I really didn't know her. When I was with her, I felt closer to being human again, than I had for a long, long time. I felt emotions that I never thought I would ever feel again. I desperately grasped at those feelings. I needed to feel alive again. I needed to feel the joys of life that I had once felt. But after one year, she left me. It was as it should be. I didn't deserve to be happy, not until I had paid for what I had done. As I recall our time together, I came to the realization that I had ruined her life. Just another life I had taken, one in many. My search and destroy missions didn't end in Vietnam, they followed me home. That's what I did. That was who I was. I was a soldier, a hardened killer. My journey continued.

I withdrew further into my dungeon. More drugs and more alcohol. In the daytime I drifted in and out of consciousness, from one world to another, and at night into the drug world. To induce sleep, I mixed drink and drugs. That took me yet, into another world. A world totally new to me and more frightening than anything I had ever experienced. It was a world that I heard talk about as a child, in Church. It was the demonic world. I was already familiar with demons, in some of my reoccurring nightmares. One that reoccurred was I was in the middle of a jungle. Not a jungle with all kinds of dense foliage, but an area where bombs and napalm had left it totally baron. It was pouring down rain as figures began to approach me. It was as a scene from "Night of the Living dead."

These figures were clad in jungle fatigues as I was. They were corpses of the dead and they were coming after me. There was no escape, so I just stood there as one of them handed me a shovel. They never spoke but somehow, I always knew what they wanted. They wanted me to dig and I refused. They began to push me from all directions. All were missing body parts and where they touched me, I began to bleed. There was no pain or wound only blood that washed down my body by the rain. I slowly began to dig but the rain washed most of the dirt back into the hole. I dug faster. I hit something hard, and saw small fingers sticking out of the dirt, a child's hand. I frantically scooped the mud away, slinging mud in all directions. I had to save her. I grabbed her hand to pull her out and her arm came off in my hand. It wasn't until years past that I realized this was a nightmare. I learned to separate nightmares from my excursions into the demonic world.

Awake or asleep, I wondered into worlds that only I visited. I needed sleep but I knew that closing my eyes would take me into the demonic world, but I had no choice. I would catch an image race across the door or a hallway, but because they were in another dimension, I couldn't really see them. But I always sensed them. I knew they were there.

When I would finally pass out, they were waiting. They never hurt me, physically. They didn't look like movie monsters, the "Alien" type. They had many human characteristics but were not pleasant to look at. The pain and fear they inflicted seemed to come with them, like a force field, an electrically charged pain and fear they seemed to radiate. This was not a world of fire, dark dreary caverns or molten lava. It was a world Inhabited by only them, no humans except for me. There were neighborhoods and houses, just like the real world. I never went inside the houses and neither did they. These were not your upscale or middle-class brick houses; these were run down shacks. They had no driveways or paved streets, just dirt. Now I know, you may ask "Where is the horror of this demonic world?" I can't answer that because I don't know, I only know that it exists. As simple as it was, I always woke up screaming and shaking, but it was my life and I accepted it.

Sometime, somewhere in my travels between my worlds, I met someone. A young lady who brought out a flicker of light in me. I reached out to her as one would reach out for life itself. We married and she gave me a child, a little girl. My Angel. I didn't know if I was capable of loving but when she was born, I knew that I was. My daughter and I went everywhere together as I desperately reached out to feel human again. But after five years, it too ended. This introduced me to a different kind of pain, a pain of losing a child. I missed my angel, dearly, but I knew she was better off without me.

My travels into the demonic world continued. Many of them, I became familiar with, in that they were present in almost every journey. Nothing was ever verbally spoken. Every communication seemed to be of a telepathic nature.

I was flashing a lot during the day. One minute in this world, next minute in the jungle. It was usually an odor, a smell that would take me back to a certain place in time. The sound of helicopters always affected me; they still do. Many times, I would hear cries in the distance, sounds that would transport me to another time. The VA would only tell me that I had combat fatigue, and that it would go away. I continued my journey.

Being unable to hold a job, I moved in with my cousin. In my struggle to regain what I could of a normal life, I again remarried. I have never said that I fell in love, because I wasn't sure what love was anymore or if I could love anyone but my children. I was desperate for life. I needed to feel again. I searched for that world because I knew it existed because I was there once. I had no idea how to have a normal relationship or even if I could have one. I loved my children deeply. I was deep into my illness and I knew it was only a matter of time. While I deeply loved my children, I knew that I had to protect them. I had to protect them from the extreme pain that comes with love. I knew what I was, and I had to protect them from me. The love for my children, no one can contest. I loved them with all that I had left. I didn't want them to hurt when I was gone because I knew death was near. All my losses in the war took a toll. Every loss took a part of me until I had nothing left. I didn't want them to suffer the way I have suffered. It was a very difficult time for me and very confusing. I longed to be back in the jungle with its dead and dying. Things were so much easier there. You killed until you were killed. Peace came with death.

The Miracle

My life continued it's downward spiral. I began to spend a lot of time in one of the worst neighborhoods in the city. It was a black neighborhood where most whites were not welcome, and the drugs flowed freely. I would walk the streets all night hoping someone would kill me. I couldn't blame my failed marriages, as I couldn't even stand myself. I spent hours in my house drugging and drinking and then one day I decided to end it. I had heard that an old friend of mine, from the hood had become a Pastor. I looked through the pages of the phone book, searching for his name. I finally found It" Pastor Joe Barrera". Joe and I had several encounters with gangs from other parts of the city. One time we were involved in a shooting at a place called the "Red Canary" where we got in a fight and three members from the other gang were shot. I knew I could depend on Joe. So, I called, and his wife answered. I asked for Joe and she said he was in the shower; this is his wife Mary Jesse and she said she would have him call me as soon as he got out. I got my shot gun and laid it across my lap. I waited for the call in which I would ask Joe to pray for me, then stick the barrel in my mouth …. And it would be over. He returned my call and I asked him to pray for me. He asked what was going on and I explained. He began to talk and told me that death was not the answer. I really didn't want to hear it, but I listened. This was on a Sunday morning and he asked me to come to Church. I argued for a while, telling him that I was in no condition to attend Church. But he said that it did not matter, come anyway. So, I did and sat out in the parking lot smoking and drinking. I finally went in and sat down feeling very uncomfortable. I took it as long as I could and walked out. A lady I had known years ago, followed me out and began to talk to me. She asked me to give God a chance. I said that I had to have a cigarette and fired one up. She begged me to go back inside and I went. I listened best I could to the sermon and then they had an altar call and asked me to come up. The Pastor and his brother Raymond, laid hands on me and prayed for me. I can already hear the non-believers denying the truth in what I say. But when they laid hands on me, I completely sobered up. All the cocaine and alcohol I had induced was waisted …… I was sober. Pastor Joe and his brother Raymond took me home and I couldn't keep my mouth shut about the miracle that took place. I began to attend Church and prayed for my children and to become sane again. I read my Bible every day, which was itself a miracle because I always found it rather boring. The urge for drugs and alcohol left and I was free for about a year. For a year I lived semi-normal and regained some normality in life. However, war experiences began to again, haunt me. All my failures and the loss of my children were re-occurring and I soon went back to my old life. The next years were worse than the beginning. I went into worlds where I had never been. There is a scripture in the Bible that explains this; Mathew 12:43-45 ….. "When an impure spirit comes out of a person, it goes through arid places seeking rest and does not find it. Then it says, "I will return to the house I left.' When it arrives, it finds the house unoccupied, swept clean and put in order. Then it goes and takes with it seven spirits more wicked than itself, and they go in and live there. And the final condition of that person is worse than the first."

Pastor Joe Barrera was my first Pastor and suffered with me through all my ordeals. I know he spent many hours praying for me. He put up with much of my drug abuse and drunkenness and never condemned me. He remains one of my oldest and dearest friends, even today.

I lost everything, I felt totally empty. A walking, breathing mass of pain. I can't begin to describe the agony and the pain. Many nights in a drunk and drugged stupor, I would paint my face with camouflage, strap on my Bowie knife and head for the woods. I roamed all night in the woods hoping that I would be magically transcended to the jungle, where I belonged. Then I would come home where the demons were waiting for my excursion into their world. I stayed drunk and ate little, settling my stomach with cocaine and pot.

I sat one day evaluating my existence. I couldn't live anymore. Every time I heard a child's voice, my heart jumped, I turned to see my children, but they were never there. My flashbacks became worse as did my nightmares. I drifted into the demonic world often. Their presence in my home was very evident to me. As I stated before, they never spoke, as some had no mouths and those that did were disfigured. There seemed to be a constant noise, a "Gibberish" coming from them always. Communication was always done by some kind of telepathic means. They seemed to never leave the house, which I found strange. The times I contemplated suicide they were never present. My communication with God was almost nonexistent but many times I asked Him to let me die. But I knew that I must pay for what I had done.

In 1988, I was admitted to the VA hospital. Besides my "World travels" I began to have severe mood swings. I was put on heavy doses of medication. These meds sent me still to another world, a world of mostly sounds, screams and voices. Many times, I crouched in the hall with my hands over my ears.

Jack

It was here that something strange began to take place. Something was happening and I didn't understand it. I began to hear another voice. The voice became a constant companion. It was very familiar and knew my every thought. It was as if I were watching a movie. Something had grown out of me…. two of me. Its name was Jack. It was as though I had known Jack all my life. Jack and I were the best of friends and very much alike. I often wondered that if by some freak hospital error, we didn't really belong to the same parents.

As children we attended the same schools as well as the same Church. We were both deeply in love with God and life. Our Church was located on a river, and as normal boys, the call of the wild often overpowered the call to Bible class. We loved to go skip rocks across the river and chunk rocks at the pigeons under the bridge. When it came close to time for Bible class to be over, we would wonder back to the Church where we would find our parents waiting for us. They would ask if we had been down at, he river again and we answered "No." We would see their eyes blaze a trail from our heads to our muddy shoes and we knew we were had. But an hour later we would be home racing across our woods, chasing behind the little animals and filling the woods with laughter. Our secret talks were often of God and all His wonders, mingled with our enthusiasms for growing up.

What seems like just a few years to me, turned into many and we were ready to leave the proverbial nest. We decided to go into the military and did just that when we turned seventeen. We enjoyed watching each other grow into manhood and sharing this part of our life together, for Jack and I were one. Our conversations had become a bit more serious since we discovered women.

Then one day a war came along and being the patriots that we were we decided to go, together. This is where I began to see the changes in Jack. As time went on, he became very distant and angry. I knew there was a war raging within him and I didn't know what to do. I saw him mutilate beings with a vengeance and hate that I can't describe. It took a constant effort to reach him. He never spoke of God anymore and I missed my old friend dearly. I felt that I was losing part of myself, for Jack and I were one. It's as though he was being possessed by something very evil and I was afraid. I could no longer read his eyes, mind or heart and I counted the days till we could leave this living hell and return home to the love and joy we had once known.

That day finally came, and I was ecstatic, but Jack never showed any emotion. I found out later that he never remembered leaving the war and returning home. Such was his state of mind. I loved and missed my old friend dearly. I tried to get him to go fishing or to the woods as we had done as children, but he refused. He never wanted to attend Church or even speak of God. He was always alone and had taken up the use of drugs and alcohol. I persistently tried to speak to him about God, but he would shut me off and say that when he had paid for what he did, God would make his life better. At times I heard him crying in his sleep, sounding like a wounded animal caught in a trap, with low whimpering cries of pain unable to escape the trap. I guess, to him, that's the way it was. One day I returned home and found him on the floor with both wrists cut. I took him to the hospital where they stitched him up and released him. This seemed to make him worse than before and at the sight of his reflection in a mirror, broke every mirror in the house. One night I was driving home, and I saw a man sitting on the steps of a nearby chapel. It was late and I wondered who that could be, so I stopped. It was Jack, drunk and drugged. Several times, I would drive by that same chapel and he would be sitting on those same steps. I begged him to let God in and he would look at me with a distant stare and say he didn't know how. I never again saw my old friend laugh or smile or even cry. It's as though he only existed, with no outward emotions. He turned away from God and all those who loved him. What he feared most was himself, but he just didn't understand. Jack didn't hate God. He believed that God hated him, so he lived a life of guilt and shame. He sentenced himself to life, without parole.

Jack disappeared one day. I often wonder about my old friend. I wonder if he kept the monster within him imprisoned or did it destroy him. I cling to the memories of our Church, our God, the river and the echoes of laughter as we ran thru the woods. But at times, when I sit and look painfully deep into the pit of my soul.... I see Jack, sitting there painfully and patiently waiting.

E.C.T. ………… Shock Therapy

I began undergoing therapy and heavy doses of medication that left me like a walking zombie. I was observed and questioned by many doctors and interns. one day my doctor approached me in a very somber mood. He told me that after careful consideration (my three suicide attempts) there wasn't much they could do for me. There was one thing left that they would like to try. It was called ECT (Electro Convulsive Therapy), better known as shock treatments. I would have one every Monday, Wednesday and Friday. I agreed since I felt death was imminent. The idea was that the electrical shocks would remove parts of my memory. After each treatment I was at a total loss. I knew no one, including myself and remembered nothing.

I finally left and went home. Thru all this, God was always there. I guess, I didn't really hate God, I hated myself. He was always trying to muscle His way back into my life, but I just wanted to be alone. As miserable as my life was, I accepted it. I deserved it. Many times, in my drunken stupors and massive drug use I could feel him, He was right there beside me. But I didn't want him there, so I continued.

One day I decided to go back to Church. Whether I was drunk, drugged or hung over, I was going. Many times, the pastor had to assign people to watch me. Of course, all I heard was how much God loves you.... Yea right! How can you love someone like me?

One day I went to jack in the box close to my home and I met a young girl. I got my order and sat down to eat. This girl came and asked if we had met before and I responded "No." She, I guessed, was in her later twenties and I was forty-five. She seemed to be attracted to me, but I passed it off as the "Young girl, older man" attraction. She introduced herself as Elvira. I have only heard that name one time in my life. Remember the old witch type woman that used to introduce the scary movies. A witch and a devil... maybe this is a good match. We didn't see each other for a while and then we met again at a friend's house. As fate would have it, we began to date and finally married. My war against God raged on. The drugs and alcohol continued. In this period of time, I was sent to Prison. It came as no surprise to me. I felt kind of at home with all the bad guys and there were fights almost daily. I spent most of my time reading. Every day we had an hour in which we could go out on the basketball court and leave our cells. The guys would always come and ask me if I wanted to go outside and I always said "No.... when I leave this cell.... I'm not coming back. They always called me Mr. Bargas. I was the only one there that they referred to as "Mr.". I thought that was strange .... But today I know that it was another "God" thing! He was always with me even though I believed that He wasn't.

I know today that God doesn't make wars; man does. I know God never hated me, I hated me. I waged a war against God that lasted more than 40 years. About five years ago, it ended. I made peace with God; I forgave myself. I tore down the walls of that self-imposed prison and let him out. I told Jack that I loved him and said, "Goodbye." I know that a soldier is always a soldier, only the enemy changes.

Sometimes people ask me what in my life I would change, if I could. My answer is always the same, "Not one thing." My journey has been long and painful. I have journeyed thru many worlds. There is but one that awaits me when the time is right.

Yes, I'm still with the girl from jack in the box, more than twenty years now. We live just a few blocks from where we first met. I want to thank my God, my wife and all those who never gave up on me. I thank all of you who read my words. God has kept His word. What the devil took, He has given back a hundred-fold. Anyone can have what I have. God made us that promise.... If you just keep trying!

ss
Bye Jack!

Book Two
The Calling

I realize today that no matter which war you fought and how far away from home it was ..... the actual battle begins here ... at home. We have the best trained Army in the world, the best equipped with the best weapons. But we are not equipped to handle what happens when we return to civilization. We can't handle the scars and memories and mental pictures that re-occur on almost a daily basis. We lost over 58,000 men in Vietnam and more than that returned home only to take their own life through suicide. This is a common occurrence with almost every war or military action that we are involved in. The rate of suicides here at home, are greater than the actual combat losses suffered overseas.

I spent more than 12 years in military hospitals and tried to take my life several times. Now, we all know that a man, who is an experienced killer, knows how to kill himself. What I was actually doing was crying out for help. When you suffer from the aftereffects of war, your ability to reason and understand properly has been diminished due to your experiences. It was only a few years ago that I realized how sick I had been. My wife and I were sitting at the kitchen table and I said, "You know...... I'm well now!" My wife looked at me in confusion and asked, "What do you mean?" I said, "I'm not sure, I just know that I've been sick for a long time and now I'm well."

People always say that war messes your head up, and since I heard it said so often, I began to believe it. Today, I know that it wasn't my head that was messed up...... it was my heart! I came home unable to feel the things that make life worth living. I was wrapped in memories of hate, pain and suffering. Flashbacks were my constant companion usually set off by a smell, a sound or scene that took me back to the jungle. My ability to love was only in a protected manner. I loved my children but because of my experiences, I had to protect them from what happened to me. I wanted them to love me but not so much that when I died, they would be destroyed. I never thought that I would live long. I knew death awaited me and it was not far off, so I had to protect them. With every friend I lost in the war, I seemed to lose a part of myself until I had nothing left but a cold heartless case. My wife asked me, before we were married, why I lived the way I did, with the drugs and drinking. She asked me if I was sure that I loved her. I told her that everyone that I loved was always taken away from me and I lived this way because when I had paid for what I did in the war...... God would make my life better. I lived in a self-imposed prison. I lived a life that I believed was the kind of life I deserved for what I had done.

I remember one of the many times I was in the VA hospital... it was therapy time and they sat me in a circle of ten or twelve doctors. They asked me how I felt, and I responded that I was alright. They said," Are you happy, sad, depressed or what?" I said that I wasn't sure what happy felt like. I wasn't sure what any of that felt like because to me, I only existed. I awaited death.

My life was a life of alcohol and drugs. But as miserable as it was, it was all that I knew. It was what I deserved. Most people don't understand that a life as I have lived ... as miserable as it is, it becomes normal and then becomes comfortable. I have heard that an amputee still feels whatever member of his body was amputated and at times still feels the pain and as inconvenient as it is ….. he becomes comfortable with it. That's the best explanation I can give you of how my life was. I accepted it because, I deserved it and through all the misery, it was normal and comfortable. After years of attending AA and NA meetings I have come to this conclusion. Alcoholism and drug addiction are not a disease as I had been told for so many years. They are "Symptoms" of deep Spiritual conflicts that lead to psychological and mental disorders. I truly believed, as I had been told, that "Once an alcoholic, always an alcoholic" and I had accepted that. But how can one explain that after I made my peace with God and myself, everything began to fall in place? Now this is not something that happened overnight. It took years of Spiritual feeding and understanding that lead to my finally being "Free". The Bible says that if we study God's word, we shall believe it ….. we shall know the TRUTH and the TRUTH shall set us FREE. Another scripture tells us that "I am the way, the TRUTH, and the life. No one comes to the Father but through me. So, if we shall know the TRUTH and the TRUTH shall set us free …. Then GOD is the Truth, and He shall set us free providing we know His word. The depression and suicidal tendencies vanished. And as I learned and believed more in God, my Spirit, itself began to heal. The urge to do drugs and alcohol all but vanished. This is why I have stated that, for years, I was treated for "Head" problems when actually I had "Heart" problems.

I always believed that God had betrayed me and abandoned me. The day of my reconning …. Was the first time that I realized that God had put Woody there for me. My dear friend and his Bible were a "Plant" that God sent and were waiting for me on my arrival. All the support and comfort he gave me and the knowledge he gave me came from God. When he died, my heart bled. In war, men don't cry … they cry, and they bleed from the inside. Woody was my Angel put there by God because He already knew what was going to happen and knew that I would need help. As much as Woody loved the Lord, I have NO doubt that he was my Angel and he never really died, he was just called back to heaven for another assignment. I can't tell you what knowing that does to my memories and pain of losing him. I can't tell you what it does to my feelings towards God. He loved me so much that He appointed Angels to be with me …. Always! The old Sarge was also an Angel …….. at least that is what I choose to believe. I know that the more than 12 years I spent in military hospitals was almost a waste of time. They spent years treating my head ….. when it was my heart that needed "Fixin".

As a child growing up, I always wondered what I was supposed to be like. I wondered what my father was like. I felt alone most of the time because I had no full-blooded relatives. Today I know that I have always known my Father ….. I just refused to see it. My Father is God. He is the ONLY person in my life that has never left me. But being unaware of that in my youth, I ran with anyone that would accept me …… Ex-cons usually. When someone would ask me what I wanted to be ….. I usually told them "An Ex-con". I began to carry a gun at a very early age and shot two people before I was 17. We stole cars and robbed stores. We fought on a regular basis. I wanted to be a tough guy. I wanted people to fear me. I wanted them to know that I was afraid of nothing. When actually ….. I was afraid of everything. I wanted people to fear me so they would leave me alone. My youth was spent with my brother Larry. I trusted him with my life, and it was during my prison time that the Lord called him home. My heart bled when I got the news ….. But I was in prison and you don't cry in prison ….. It's a weakness…… and will be used against you. Larry was another of my "Angels" and when his job was finished….. God called him home. I always thought that we would grow old together, but God had other plans for him and me both. At times…. Even today… I weep for him and my heart longs just to hear his voice and see him smile.

We grew up in a very difficult time. A time of extreme racism with black and white-water fountains and restrooms. A time when we could not eat in white restaurants and had to sit at the back of the bus. Schools were segregated and everyone was judged by your skin color. Racism still exists today, only it is well hidden most of the time. As a Hispanic we usually drank from the black water fountain and used the black restrooms. They seldom said anything to us to where the white people would usually tell us we didn't belong there ……. So, we used what was available and where we felt most welcome.

The New Beginning

I was growing tired of Pastors and Churches. There seemed to be little difference. My wife took a job selling insurance and became good friends with a lady named Loraine Williams. She often spoke of her and what a good Christian she was. My idea of a GOOD Christian seemed to be something of the past. It seems that Lorraine's husband had retired from the military and was opening a church just a few blocks from our house. They were remodeling the building and she asked if I wanted to go with her to see it. I really didn't …… but I told her I would just to be nice. When we arrived, I saw that they were putting in carpet and painting the walls. Lorrain's husband was there, and we were introduced. We had a conversation in which I told him I was a Vietnam veteran. We began to speak about Churches and God, and I told him I was a little tired of searching for the truth and no one seemed to know what the truth is. I spoke of how the Bible says you are to love everyone, and I don't even like most people. There are two words that I don't take lightly, one is "Friend and the other is Christian" They seem to be tossed around freely as if they mean nothing. I listened to his responses. He seemed to be genuine, intelligent and seemed to be overloaded with compassion. I wasn't one for much compassion. I wondered why he would want to be a Pastor. I told him that you could not pay me enough to be a Pastor. I just wasn't made for that. I couldn't sit and listen to everyone's problems ….. I have enough of my own. And my experiences have shown me that very few people take advice from anyone they just continue doing what they please, so why waste your time. And then the name of the Church was Divine Connection Ministries. I didn't tell the Pastor, but it was a real "sissy" name. I mean I'm a man of war, raised in the barrio and the word "Divine" is not in my vocabulary. Can you imagine .... "Hey Homie, how you like my new Stacy's Vato?" "Oh, they're just Divine" .... Get what I mean? But anyway ..... There seemed to be a pleasant "Strangeness" in this man as I devoured his every word. We had been attending another Church and I didn't particularly want to change .... I mean .... There isn't that much difference. My wife said that the Lord had placed it in her heart to attend this church and help them build a congregation. I told her that I was not changing churches again. Several months went by and my conversation with the Pastor kept re-playing in my mind. His words seemed to haunt me. So, I decided to give this new church a chance. It was a multi-cultural church...... all colors. I enjoyed the sermons and found myself laughing a lot. I hoped the Pastor would not think I was laughing at him and be offended. It was humorous to me because he was so direct with his words .... No "Sugar Coating". You were free to disagree with him and being the outspoken person that I was ...... I often did .... In private. He would patiently take me to scripture to back up what he said. I began to learn that much of what other churches were preaching was not exactly what was contained in scripture and a lot was just plain compromise. I found the people a little strange too. They seemed to really care about you. They accepted me with all my character defects and short comings and really loved me and that was not something I was used to. I began to realize how sick and empty I had been for so many years. I began to really care about people and have compassion. Many times, my eyes watered up when hearing people's confessions and I really didn't care much for that. At times I wanted to be the "Old" hard me, that wasn't bothered by someone else's problems. It became common for me to do that "Cry Baby" stuff. For many years I heard about God and I got tired of hearing about God. What I wanted was "Show me God". Show me God in you. I wanted to be able to point at someone and say, "The God he has is the God I want." .... I finally found that! For years I met people who told me about God and then I would see them outside of church and suddenly they weren't acting or speaking like they did when they were in church. Many times, it was a "Money" situation. I often thought "What happened to Jesus"? I came to the conclusion that if being a Christian, is being like them ...... I don't want it. But this Pastor and people were different. I understand, today, that Church is a hospital for sick people, and you go there to get healed, not because you are perfect. These people accepted me for who I was because they saw .... what I could be! I'll be forever grateful for that!

Here's a very brief run down: My life was nothing to be proud of. I never knew my biological father and my mom left me with my grandma for a few years when she re-married. I remember wondering what was wrong with me, that made people not want me. I remember crying for my Mom and wondering about my Father. I began to roam the streets and began carrying a gun at twelve. I shot two people before I was 16, stole cars and robbed stores, fought in gangs and drugged and drank. Went to a war and became a real killer. Came home and spent more than 12 years in military hospitals, had a series of 18 shock treatments, tried to kill myself many times, 3 times

That are on record, became a drunk and drug addict, spent many nights in jails of several states and went to prison. I hated God for more than 40 years, tried to go back to church but I knew that God didn't want me. I didn't like any one and had no friends, but I didn't want any. Now … suddenly, my life has changed.

Today my friends come in all colors because we are ALL of one race …… the human race. I have Angels of all colors. My most recent one came to me about a year ago. His name is Lafayette Williams …. he is my Pastor. He reminded me of Woody since they were both so soft spoken, patient and both loved God. I toyed with the fact that he might be Woody…… re-incarnated. He tells me I'm to love everyone, which is still difficult for me. It reminded me of the time Woody was trying to tell me that man makes war…….. not God.

Today's Wars

As I stated previously, we have all fought wars. There are physical, combat wars and those that are fought at home. Since I have become a Christian, I realize that there are still many wars to be fought. Not only the wars of temptation from sin but the wars that exist within our nation. Becoming a Christian is only the beginning. To be successful in our battles doesn't mean pray and fast. We must take action, or nothing changes. Praying and having Faith is only the beginning. We must stand up for our beliefs. I have found that most Christians are not people of action. They are comfortable going to Church and praying for things to change and the fact is that they seldom change without some kind of action being taken. In most Churches I have attended it is hard to even get volunteers to come and help clean the Church much less to go out on the streets and evangelize. Most people don't care to go door knocking and spread the word of God. We won't pressure the school districts to put prayer back in school or the entertainment industry to take the trash off of the theaters or our TV sets. We don't get involved in the gun issues, drugs, school shootings, drive byes or human trafficking. All these things exist because there is money to be made. Even celebrity Preachers act like it doesn't exist or it is someone else's problem. All they care about is bringing in the money because their kids are in private schools their homes are well guarded and money buys security, while the common man still suffers the effects of all this crime. So where exactly is God in this picture? The problems of my brothers are also my problems because life isn't just about me, it's about us! I hear Preachers speaking about the state of our Nation, road rage, school shootings and crime, but they do nothing but talk! The first step begins with you! They are the shepherds that are supposed to take care of the sheep. ……. Jeremiah 23:1 …. "Woe to the shepherds who are destroying and scattering the sheep of my pasture.!" Declares the Lord. Therefore, this is what the Lord, the God of Israel, says to the shepherds who tend my people," Because you have scattered my flock and driven them away and have not bestowed care on them, I will bestow punishment on you for the evil you have done, "declares the Lord. (NIV).

America: Home of the Brave and Land of the Free

Is it really? I remember as a child reciting the Pledge of Allegiance every morning at school. The most important part read like this:" One Nation, under God, indivisible, with Liberty and justice for all. I wonder what happened. We have become a Godless Nation. A nation divided between the left and the right, black and white, democrats and republicans, conservatives and liberals. When it's time to elect our representatives, we vote for what has become the lesser of two evils. Can you remember when we could actually vote for someone who Truly represented our Godly beliefs? I pick the guy I like the least and vote for the other guy.

We have a lot of celebrity preachers with millions and sometimes billions in their bank accounts and not one will seek public office. Not one will step forward and, with God's help' try and change the path of our nation. What happened to the "Boldness" the Bible speaks of that they echoed from the pulpit every Sunday? Every Sunday they are on the tube preaching about how we need to put God back into America, but they want someone else to do it, cause they're too busy making money. They talk about pornography, suicides, road rage and school shootings and as soon as the program ends ….. their interests end and they go home to their mansions. Liberty and justice for all …. We don't even have the freedom to send our children to school and know they will be safe or drive down the street and know you won't be gunned down by some *road rage idiot who has a 9-millimeter and doesn't even need a permit to carry it. They don't even have sense enough to understand that "weapons of War" are just that< for war not the streets. Justice is "Color Coded", and racism is alive and well. If your eyes aren't round and your skin not white, you are "Substandard". There is but ONE race. The people we elect to office find hundreds of ways to divide us. They lie to us so much that even We don't know the truth. So, we go to Church to hear God's word and the real truth and the churches are telling us who to vote for so, maybe, they can get millions in PPP loans. If we, as Christians, don't like what one church preaches, we find another who will tell us what we want to hear, so when we leave, we can go home with a cheerful heart. THE TRUTH is BITTER and hard to swallow, just like most medicines but it is the only thing that will make us well. We have become a twisted, Godless and selfish nation and I am ashamed. But the real shame lies on the heads of all the money preachers who claim they fight against evil and claim Faith and tell us faith is an action word ….. so, where is their action. We're just supposed to believe, pray and send money and things will get better. They don't spend a dime or lift a hand to change a nation that is caught up in SIN…….. ONE NATION UNDER GOD INDIVISIBLE, WITH LIBERTY AND JUSTICE FOR ALL…….. what happened.*

All that is needed for evil to prevail is for good men to sit and do nothing ……. That is exactly the example that they set!

On some of my "Witnessing "experiences I have asked people if they have a church, or do they believe in God and do you believe God will meet your needs and most say yes.

If they have no home church, I invite them to ours and tell them the service is at 9AM. Immediate turn off "Oh that's too early, I like to sleep late." So, as not to be rude I suggest they visit on Wednesday Bible study. But what I want to say is" didn't you just say that you believe in God, you have Faith, that God died for our sins and He has provided for you?" You are blessed with a good job, your health your children, but that's too early for you? You get up early for work, trips, special events, but going to church is not a special event and you get paid for work. Is it all a lie? Can you tell your children that you love them and not do anything for them, but you expect God to believe you love Him ...... just don't ask so much of me? This is a hypocritical lifestyle, and we are a spoiled, hypocritical, lazy nation. We want to sit in bed and eat breakfast while we watch it all on TV. Wake up! Life is not about you.

I have been confused, drunk, drugged, no vision, tired, bored and lost. Every day now I wake up excited, full of life with visions you cannot imagine and it's all because God changed my heart. Every day I want to tell everyone how great life is. We're getting our house remodeled, paid off both cars.... All this since God changed my life. I have told people this and they are happy for me, or they say they are, and they ask how did you do it? YOU SAY GOD DID IT AND THIER EXPRESSION CHANGES. IT'S LIKE I JUST TOLD THEM I HAD THE COVID.

As we approach another year, we must all enter with a dream, a vision for a better year. Part of my dream is included in the following: "I have a dream that my four children will live in a nation where they will not be judged by the color of their skin, but by the content of their character. I have a dream. I have a dream that every valley shall be exalted, every hill or mountain be made low, the rough places will be made will be made plain and the crooked places will be made straight, and the Glory of the Lord shall be revealed, and all flesh shall see it together. This will be the day when all of God's children will be able to sing, with a new meaning, "My country tis of thee, sweet land of liberty, of thee I sing. Land where my fathers died, land of the Pilgrims pride, from every mountainside, let freedom ring." And if America is to be a great Nation, this must become true. So, let freedom ring from the prodigious hilltops of New Hampshire. Let freedom ring from the mighty mountains of New York. Let freedom ring from the heightening Alleghenies of Pennsylvania, from Stone mountain of Georgia, from Lookout mountain of Tennessee and from every hill and molehill of Mississippi. And when this happens, when we allow freedom to ring from every village, and every hamlet, from every state and every city, we will be able to speed up that day when all God's children, black and white men, Jews and Gentiles, Protestants and Catholics, will join hands and sing that old negro Spiritual "Free at last, free at last, thank God Almighty we are free at last."…. August 28th, 1963 Dr. Martin Luther King.

I am not speaking solely of freedoms from divisions, whether it is one's color, Faith, political preference or country of origin. We must forgive … to be forgiven ….. love …. To be loved.. We must build our states and cities from Faith and Love, build our Churches on Biblical Truths and principles, and not by color and compromise. We must build our communities not by cultural differences but by cultural contributions and live our lives as brothers … not enemies. We must exalt every valley with Praise, lower every mountain with Faith and straighten every crooked road with God's word. Only then will we be able to say, "In God We Trust." Only then can we transform the jangling discords of our nation into "A beautiful Symphony of Brotherhood" "We must all learn to live together as brothers or perish together as Fools" …. IT IS TIME!

Last night we had a leadership meeting at Church and when we came home my wife began to run through a list of names of people, we needed to buy gifts for. For some reason this took me back in time …. A time when I lived alone and would go out and buy enough drugs and alcohol to last me for months. I often went weeks without speaking a word or leaving the house. I had no friends and didn't want any. Three weeks ago, I turned 75. I didn't receive many gifts, but I don't place a lot of value on gifts because I had one of the greatest gifts already … I had lived for 75 years and I had a chance to change my life and experience TRUE life, as God intended.

I left the meeting a little saddened. My Pastor said some things we need to do for the upcoming year. As he spoke, he told of what God had put in his heart, of ways to reach more people and as he usually does, he gave God all the Glory. Well…. I'm all for that but here is what I have to say …… Don't sell yourself short …. You have read all that I have written, and it continued into my marriage. And most of my life. There's an old saying, "You can lead a horse to water, but you can't make him drink." Many Pastors have led this old horse to water, but none made him drink! I didn't begin to attend that church because of God …. My Pastor led me to water, and I drank …. I drank because of this strange Pastor and his compassion for people, his love of God and his truth in the word. He didn't make me read the Bible ….. I read it because I wanted what he had. Last month we missed some church due to illness and when we returned the Pastor called us up front. He told of how we were missed and how glad they were to have us back. My mind was wrestling with what I was hearing. Why would anyone miss me and glad to have me back as I am very outspoken and not very compassionate? People stood and clapped and said they loved us as tears streamed my face. My grandbabies walk up to me and hugs my waist. She says, "Hug me Pawpaw and She lifts her little face to look at me and says, "I love you Paw paw" and I'm overwhelmed with Love. Who could love this Godless, loveless man? This is the greatest gift anyone could have given me …. A new life … And it was my Pastor who made it all possible. Yes, God did it, but it was my Pastor who led me there and made it all possible or I might still be living in that world of darkness. The greatest gifts in life don't come in boxes wrapped in pretty paper ….. they come from the heart wrapped in love and my Pastor gave me that!

There are times when I want to miss church, usually due to a good football game which interferes with it. But I know that whatever my Pastor's message …. I need to hear it. I re-posted some old posts from FB yesterday because as I read them, I realized I was slipping a little. One was about love and loving everyone as Christ did … even Peter who had betrayed Him. Another was about being the head, which is another hard one for me. I had to remind myself of what is pleasant to God and not to me. After a while I begin to slip and some of the old begins to creep back in and I need a refresher. Church helps me stay alert. It's my training camp where I'm fed properly, corrected and my mistakes are pointed out. It's where I'm reminded whose will and whose plans are more important. It's where I'm reminded that life, isn't about me and I'm' reminded of that person who "talks about everybody or the one who lies all the time and the one who is so prideful that I can't stand ...... could be a "Mirror". How about those hypocritical preachers or those congressmen who can't tell the TRUTH .... Are they "Mirrors"? That's why I need Church, not only to thank and praise God but I need those "Cataracts" from a week of living in a sinful world .... Removed. I want to see clearly and truthfully.

I have a Confession

Ever been in a room with people where you're trying to say something, and some are listening, and others are having their own conversations? But the minute you say "I have a confession …. The entire room is quiet! All ears are "Perked" and they can't wait to hear what you did wrong.

Well, last night, I was a little tired and I got a glass of ice, poured me a coke, went to my room, fluffed up my 6 pillows and laid back with my Roku remote ready to enjoy a good movie. Suddenly there's a knock at the door …. You know the door to your heart. I didn't want to answer because I knew who it was, and when He comes that late, it's never something that I want to hear. I ignored it. But it was persistent….. so, I finally answered. He said," Some have called you a man of God." (I had been thinking about that earlier.) "People have praised your writing …. What do you think? "To make a long story short ….. He had me perform "Open Heart Surgery", right there and then. He was telling me that even though I was on the right track, …….. "Don't get comfortable." The race has only begun. I immediately got this mental picture of a Cowboy game I once saw, years ago, where the running back was going in for a touchdown. The crowd cheered him on as he approached the goal line and confident of a touch down he began to slow down ….. but what he failed to see was the defender that was sneaking up behind him and suddenly the ball was slapped out of his hand. There was no touch down and the game was lost.

How many of us confess to being Christians (meaning Christ like) and begin the race to the goal line and begin to slow down, only to have the ball slapped out of our hand. We go to church every Sunday and Wednesday; read our Bible and we think we have a touchdown. What about our hearts? Jesus walked this earth and everything He went through was for us. We go to church and read our Bibles but what do we do for others? Being Christ like is not about us. Because of my hard life, I have never been a man with a lot of compassion and I still need work in that area. But when I began attending church, I sat in the front row, and when the Pastor had an alter call, I found myself feeling the pain of the people that went up for prayer. I really didn't like that. When we go evangelize, I find myself feeling their pain as my compassion rises. Going to church, being involved in church, reading our Bibles is not enough … that is only beginning the race. I know people who have gone to church for years. They are leaders in the church and attend church regularly, and probably read their Bibles, but they have slowed down thinking they are at the goal line, something serious happens and they get the ball slapped out of their hand. Making a touch down is a Team effort. It's about all of us making a touchdown. Being ex military …. You never leave a comrade behind. It's not about us, it's about them. You never leave a comrade behind …. You drag him or carry him across the goal line. Don't get comfortable listening to the cheers and slow down and don't cross the goal line alone. My purpose in writing isn't money or fame ….. it's to take you and you with me. So, you can have what I have.

Five Minutes Away From Death

It's 4:50 Tuesday morning. My Pastor came home last night. I have missed him and my First Lady. In the past two days, I have met 5 of my Grandchildren, of which 4 of them, I have never seen. They are all adults now. As I lay in bed, I thought about a scripture .... "Delight yourself in the Lord, and He will give you the desires of your heart. Then you will take delight in the Lord, and He will answer your prayers." Psalms 37:4 .... I have never thought much about this scripture, even though I have heard it most of my life. But I have been experiencing what that scripture said .... The promises of God. I have found that He does keep His promises. I'm up early this morning because I'm excited about my Pastor and meeting my Grandchildren. But I was awakened by a dream, and in that dream, I saw a man lying face down in the living room of the Polo Club Apartments. I heard his mothers voice, tearfully telling the ambulance driver to rush him to the Veterans hospital. I heard the ambulance driver say, "Ma'am, we have to get him to the nearest hospital or in 5 minutes he could be dead." This wasn't the first attempt it was the third. That was me laying there dying. What if God had let Satan have me? What if God had grown tired of my hate and disobedience and just given up? All the joys of my Church, my Pastor, my friends, my grandchildren, my marriage ..... everything would have never happened. I would have been lost to a life in hell. Needless to say, that my focus in those days had nothing to do with God. It had nothing to do with enjoying worldly things. I was so wrapped up in pain and memories and my life had no purpose. I existed wrapped in all my pain, memories, drugs, alcohol and could care less if I lived or died. But God, in all His mercy, had a plan and was not willing to let Satan have me. I awakened every morning, if I got any sleep at all, dreading another day. I always preferred the night … it helped me hide …. From people and from God. I saw no beauty in anything, food had no flavor, the sun had no light, flowers had no beauty, and I had no hope. Does that sound like you? My God has kept all His promises….. yes, the same God I have cursed, hated and never believing a word that was written … has, in all His Mercy fought Satan and declared "You cannot have him!" And here I am today … alive and healed! I see beauty ever where, I love the day filled with white clouds and blue skies, the smell of flowers and the beauty of the butterflies. I love everyone and I love life….. yet I still see the man lying on the carpet and my heart goes out to him ….. for it's not me, anymore, it is someone else. There is but one answer and that is GOD. I'm not here to Preach, only to pass on my experiences so that maybe I can save a life or improve a life with the hope that there can be a better life, if you just call on Him. It doesn't come all at once, but it does come. He doesn't come to you like a roaring lion …. He'll come to you with a Whisper. A whisper to your heart … that there is a better way. Even if it's only for a moment … give Him a chance. I promise that you can have what I have with just a little bit of work. It's that or the man on the floor. Trapped in a self-imposed prison … while God is holding his hand out saying, "here are the keys, release yourself and follow me." This comes to you, not from a Preacher, but from someone just like you. A message of Hope! Reach out and take the keys!

Christianity Today

Bringing in the New Year made me do a lot of searching. Soul searching within me and within the "Christian Establishment". We had the usual big family gatherings at our house and enjoyed a Fiest for two days. But my nights, when I do most of my soul searching, were troubled. I wondered why our Christmas and New Years celebrations always included alcohol. Now, you have read about my alcoholic past, so I don't condemn entirely condemn alcohol. Some people enjoy a little wine with their meals but that isn't what I saw. As we gathered to celebrate the Birth of our Lord, I saw a table covered with alcohol. I questioned if the celebration was really for the Lord's Birthday or was it just a celebration. I feel that celebration of the New Year should be done as a day in which the old is passed away and the new is implemented. But what I saw was the "Old" being introduced as the new. There was no difference. It was just brought over from last year. This made me not only question my Christian walk but question everyone who professes to be a Christian. How can we celebrate the Birth of Christ with a glass of alcohol on the table? How can we show gratitude for the last year or even Bless the food with a table covered with alcohol? How can you say you are a Christian while you mix your third Margarita? There were those of us who chose not to indulge, who believed it a little "Improper". I said nothing because I, myself, was not indulging, so I was not guilty of anything. But as I replayed the scene within the walls of my mind that night, I realized that I was part of everything that transpired. What I saw was a group of people going in to rob a Bank,

But I was not involved in the actual bank robbery, because I only drove the "getaway car."

As I lay there viewing mental pictures as they bounced off the walls of my mind, I thought about the military. I wanted to be an Airborne soldier because I loved their appearance, and I didn't want to be just a "Regular". Soldier, I wanted more. When I entered the Labor Force, I didn't want to be just a regular employee, I wanted to be at the top. We all do. Even if you begin flipping burgers, you want to become a shift leader and hopefully advance to a manager's position, so the more you learn the better the odds for advancement. You don't want to be a Bank teller all your life, you want to advance to a Branch Manager. You don't want to join a large corporation never to, someday, advance to the CEO position. So, the more you know, the better the chance for advancement and the better the pay. So why is it not the same way with Christianity? People may quite getting drunk as often as they used to, quit cussing and maybe smoking. They begin to attend Church, when they can, and they think they have arrived. Christianity should be the, at least, the same as any job. The more we learn, the better the odds for advancing to the top. Needless to say, Christianity is far more important than any job, it is a matter of Life and Death. But it seems that most people only want" Enough" of God as long as it doesn't interfere with our worldly pleasures. I want more. I want God to remove the cataracts of life and compromise and make me a General in His Army. I want to be able to distinguish between what is contrary to His word and what is compromise. Christianity means Christ Like. Jesus gave His life for us; He didn't give just a little and say, "That's enough." He gave it all. I often see these quizzes on Facebook where you touch the tongue, and it tells you about yourself. Or you are asked what colors you see first and they tell you about yourself. They should have a quiz with questions that tell you what kind of a Christian you are. It would be interesting to see how many really take it …… how many really want to know!

The Dream

I woke up about three this morning after a dream about my life. Those of you who know me already know about my life, those of you who don't ...... it hasn't been a good one. I have always hated being afraid of something so every fear in my life .... I confronted. I grew up wanting to be bad like the ex-cons I used to run with. So, I knew that sooner or later I must go to prison ...... and I did. I was also afraid of heights, so when I joined the military, I decided to become a paratrooper. Not only did they have the best uniforms, but I needed to be rid of this fear. This is what I found ..... After the war, I got really bad. The war really messed my head up. I would ask God to take away the drugs, alcohol, anger and pain but with no results. But He can't take away something you aren't willing to give up. I decided to start going to Church, whether I was drunk, hung-over or drugged, I was going to Church on Sunday. I realize today that I was doing and asking for all the wrong things. The war didn't mess my head up, it messed my heart up, I was Spiritually dead. When I went to war, I made up my mind that I would die for my country and my beliefs, if need be. I wrote a small piece in my book that said, "Bind me hand and foot and cast me into the pit of hell and I shall still be free. Freedom is a thing of the heart just as love is. Things of the heart cannot be taken away. You lose them only if you choose to give them up. No one can take away my love for my children, my wife, my grandbabies or God .... But I can give them up. I asked God to give me love and understanding for people so that I may control the words of my tongue. If the tongue is the messenger of the heart, then I am asking the wrong thing. I need my heart cleansed. You don't need to change the way you think if you just change your heart. Your heart will convict you and you will make the necessary changes. You're drinking and alcohol problems are symptoms of a heart condition, not a disease. Your loneliness, depression and hopeless life are symptoms of a heart condition. Fix your heart which is your Spiritual life, and you fix it all.

The Final Summary

I have stated that we all have wars all trough our lifetime. Divorce is very traumatic for children and they may grow with many character flaws from such trauma. Deaths may scar you for life, creating many unwanted character traits. The wars of living accompany everyone's life. That is why we need someone with the power to heal our broken hearts. That someone is God. But there are conditions that must be met. After the war, I became very hostile, the memories, pain and anger were ever present, and my mother kept telling me to give it to God. I always told her that I had tried that, and God just didn't want them. I was raised in the Church and I knew God. Here is the "Kicker"...... I knew of God but didn't really know God.

When I married my wife, I married her because I loved her and wanted to spend the rest of my days with her. After we were married and lived together, I found that I didn't really know her the way I thought I did. Dating allows only a limited amount of time spent together. We had many negative encounters. Today, 23 years later, I can truthfully say I know her. It's the same way with God. I knew God but I had no relationship. I experienced God every Sunday, but I NEVER LIVED WITH HIM! I spent more than 50 years living in a self-imposed prison. I sentenced myself to life without parole for something that God had forgiven me for the first time I said, "Forgive me Lord." I had many brief emotional feelings but never had a lasting encounter with God. When the feelings passed, so did God. I never lived with Him.

Churches today are filled with people who, as I did, have many emotional Godly feelings but they are brief and when they leave Church, they leave God. I've spoken to many people who profess to be Christians but they still party with alcohol and drugs. I've spoken to people who attend Church and have not grown in 20 years, but they love their Pastor. Salvation is not about a close relationship with your Pastor, it's about a close relationship with God. Your Pastor will not get you saved! Those brief Spiritual feelings that make you feel the presence of God are only a taste of what god can give you when you establish a life in Christ that has no end and can last forever. But most people seem to be more interested in the in dating or brief encounters because anything more would call for a change of life and they aren't willing to give that up. There is nothing in this world that can give you what God can give you. It doesn't come in pill size, in a syringe or in a bottle. Stop living the life you think you deserve. Stop limiting yourself based on what you think you should have. What God has to offer is unmatched.

Most of todays Churches preach a watered- down version of the word of God. They are there to make people feel comfortable and not to offend. The true word of God never offends. Being offended comes from conviction and guilt because you are hearing something that you don't want to hear or deal with. The true word of God is not easy to swallow at times and is even harder to achieve in your actions because of what we have been accustomed to in the past. You will not find the true word of God in most Churches. You must seek the truth of the word yourself and you must cross reference and dig in order to find the truth. You cannot read the Word as you do a regular book. Every time I read over a text, I discover a new meaning. All my life I have heard of the Living Bible. I have heard that the word of God is alive. Old Wives Tales is what it was to me. Not too long ago, when I was in a very dark place, I cried out to God and He answered. That day as I sat on the sofa and my wife came to sit beside me, I told her something that I was dealing with. I didn't tell her when it happened because I thought she would think I had been drinking or that I was just lying. I said:" I don't know if you are going to believe this but I'm going to tell you anyway. All my life I have heard that the word of God is alive ..... the living Bible, and I always thought it was someone's over exaggeration … or it came from some "Jesus Freak" …. But something happened to me the other day. Do you remember when we had that little argument and you left to go do something. I was really upset. I began to dwell on what happened and suddenly I felt a tugging that told me to read my Bible. So, I went to my bed and got my Bible and began to read. This, unexplainable peace came over me. I read for hours. The strange thing was that the words came to life as if they were alive and moving. This frightened me some. I thought I might be having a stroke or something. But I couldn't because I had total peace and was not feeling ill. As I continued to read, I felt as if I was digesting the words ..... Yes …. I was eating the words. You may not believe what I am saying but it is the truth." My wife looked at me and said," do you remember what was prophesied over you. She said you would be eating the word of God." My wife had recorded the session and she replayed it so I could hear it. The prophesy was word for word of what I had just told her. Now, many of you are probably thinking what I always thought ……. "Another Religious Nut!" But what I said …..

really happened ..... even now, as I write and replay it in my mind...... it seems almost impossible. I know today ...... that there are no limits to the miracles of God.

I remember a time in Vietnam, when we had an ambush set up along a well-used trail overlooking a stream. Charlie kept coming and one by one we kept killing. Then we saw three Charlies appear and stopped at the stream. They looked up at the woods in the direction of our ambush. They seemed to have a brief conversation and crossed the creek headed towards our position. Two of them walked towards our position as the other veered off to the left. I was standing behind a tree and my comrade was laying at the base of the tree and we had a bead on the two approaching Cong. As they approached us, we opened up with automatic fire and they went down, when suddenly I heard a tig break to our right and as I swung around, I saw the third man ready to heave a grenade at us. I pulled the trigger and my weapon misfired But Tony, the guy laying by the tree swung around and gunned him down. We approached the dead Cong and found a grenade in his hand with the pin halfway out. We came very close to dying.

It was a dark and rainy night. We were dug in and had been fighting for days. I left my foxhole to check on some new recruits that had just arrived. As I stood trying to comfort them, I heard a barrage of incoming mortar rounds. There was no place for me to hide so I just hit the ground. I heard a round coming but no explosion. In the war, there's an old saying that if you hear the round coming...... it's for you. The next morning, I went back to check on the men and I found the round that was meant for me. It was stuck in the ground two feet from where I had been laying the night before …… unexploded.

In my twelve years in military hospitals, I had been sent to the VA hospital in Waco Texas. I remember being in my room and suddenly I had a dream ….. for lack of a better word. The catch was that I was wide awake. ….. I was standing out on the balcony of a house. This house was like they had in the south during the times when they had plantations. It was a large white house with a balcony over the front porch standing on large round pillars. I remember the hopeless feeling and the feeling to end my life. I walked to the edge of the balcony when I was grabbed from behind. I only saw two arms in a white, what appeared to be a robe, wrapped around me as I went over the edge to my death as I hit the ground. Somehow, when I landed, I landed on top of the person who obviously was trying to stop me from jumping. I stood and looked at the ground. There was a white robe with nothing in it. I couldn't figure how I could be dreaming when I was wide awake. I called my wife (my girlfriend then) and I told her of the dream. She still remembers it.

My purpose for telling this is to make known that when God has a plan for your life ……. He will protect you from Satan and any demonic plagues that attack you. At this point in time, I still never believed that anyone could have your life planned. I'm sure as you read my experiences that your own life reflected instances that were unexplainable then, as they are now. Don't underestimate God. Know that God has a plan for your life. Know that your life can be changed just as mine has been. Know that there is hope and that you don't have to live your life struggling to to survive in loneliness, with no peace, and no direction, believing that God has abandoned you. The war in Vietnam was nothing compared to the Spiritual war we fight here at home. The darkness that I lived in so many years disabled me from remembering the times Larry and I laid by the river riverbank, our poles in the water, watching the clouds roll by and talking about nothing important. I never recalled the times I laid in the tall grass by my railroad track or skipping rocks across the river when we should have been in Bible class. I never thought about my parents and sisters, as we lay around the TV, the soothing words of my Grandmother as she served us cookies and milk and spoke of old bandido times in old Mexico. Darkness steals all your peaceful memories and replaces them with hopelessness, depression and confusion. Depression is not a disease as doctors have labeled it ……. It is the absence of God. Put God in your heart and those memories and more, will come again with your children and grandchildren, but you must fight this war and you must win. The only victory comes from God. All the symptoms I suffered, suicide, depression, alcohol, drugs and the rage and pain were all symptoms of a Godless life! Know that there is a God, and He is waiting for you. He won't come with trumpets blaring, but as a whisper in the night as He touches your heart. Open the door and invite Him in. You have read my life ………. What I have now is yours for the asking.

Christmas
'1967'
Republic of Vietnam
AIRBORNE